The Last Lama Warrior

The Last
LAMA WARRIOR

The Secret Martial Art of Tibet

Yogi Tchouzar Pa

Translated by Jack Cain

Destiny Books
Rochester, Vermont

Destiny Books
One Park Street
Rochester, Vermont 05767
www.DestinyBooks.com

Destiny Books is a division of Inner Traditions International

Originally published in French under the title *Le Dernier Lama Guerrier* by
    Presses du Châtelet, 34, rue des Bourdonnais, 75001 Paris
First U.S. edition published in 2009 by Destiny Books

Library of Congress Cataloging-in-Publication Data
Pa, Yogi Tchouzar.
  [Dernier lama guerrier. English]
  The last lama warrior : the secret martial art of Tibet / Yogi Tchouzar Pa ;
translated from the French by Jack Cain.
      p. cm.
  First published in French as *Le dernier lama guerrier* by Presses du Châtelet.
  Includes bibliographical references and index.
  ISBN 978-1-59477-285-6 (pbk.)
  1. Martial Arts—China—Tibet. 2. Martial arts—Religious aspects. I. Cain,
Jack, 1940– II. Title.
  GV1100.7.T54P3 2009
  796.8—dc22
                                                            2009005181

Printed and bound in the United States of America by Lake Book Manufacturing

10 9 8 7 6 5 4 3 2 1

Illustrations and calligraphy by Yogi Tchouzar Pa
Thangkas and bronze from Tibet courtesy of the Rigden Collection
Photographs courtesy of the Association Sengueï Ngaro

Text design and layout by Jon Desautels
This book was typeset in Garamond Premier Pro with Tiepelo as display typeface

To Shambhala's rulers
The great bodhisattvas,

To the fierce and powerful Rudra Chakrin
Lord of wailing and tears on the turning wheel,

To King Ling Gesar
The valiant messenger of peace,

To all the khampa *riders*
The fearless horsemen now long gone,

To His Holiness the Dalai Lama
The ruler wielding boundless compassion,

To the regents of the noble lineages
Precious guides in the dharma,

To the lama *warriors*
The guardians of Sengueï Ngaro,

To the snow lioness
Shining white protectress of Tibet.

I dedicate this book.

YOGI TCHOUZAR PA

སྙིང་རྗེ་གི་ཉིན་འཁྲོ་བཙུགས་པ་བརྒྱགས་སོ།

༄༄། །སེམས་ཅན་ཐམས་ཅད་བདག་སངས་རྒྱས་འཐོབ་པའི་ཕྱིར། །

དཀོན་མཆོག་གསུམ་ལ་སྐྱིང་ནས་སྐྱབས་སུ་མཆི། །

ན་མོ་པུ་ཏྟེ་ བཛྲ་སྤུ་ཊེ་ཡ། །

དགེ་ལ་ཡིད་རང་ཆོས་བསྐོར་ཞིང་བཞུགས། །

ཀུན་ཏུ་བཟང་པོ་ཡིན་པོ་བསྐུལ་བར་ཤོག །

ཆོས་ཉིད་མི་འགྱུར་སྐུང་བ་མཐའ་བལ་ཞེ། །

འགགས་མེད་སྐྱེ་རྗེ་ཡོངས་སྐྱོང་སྤྲུན་རས་གཟིགས། །

ཨོ་རྒྱན་པད་ཆེན་རྣུས་སྐྲེས་སྤྲུལ་པའི་སྐུ། །

གསོལ་བ་འདེབས་སོ་ཤེན་དོན་བར་ཆད་བསལ། །

འཆེ་ཁ་ནད་འབྱུང་སྤྱག་བསལ་མི་འབྱུང་ཞིང་། །

ཚོ་འདི་སྐྱང་བ་ནུབ་པའི་སྐྱེ་མ་དག །

བདེ་བ་ཅན་གྱི་རེ་པོ་པོ་དུ་ལྷ། །

ཐབས་མདོག་དཔལ་གྱི་རེ་པོ་སྐྱིས་བར་ཤོག །

ཨོ་ཨ་མེ་བདེ་ཧཱི། །ཨོ་ཨ་ཏི་པུརེ་ཚོ་ཉི་སྭ། །

ཨོ་ཨ་ཚོ་བཛྲ་གུ་རུ་པདྨེ་སིདྡྷི་ཚོ། །

སེང་གེའི་དེ་རོ་སྐྱ་ཆེ་ཤུན་རེ་བརྟན་པར་ཤོག །

སེང་གེའི་དེ་རོ་བསྐུན་འགྲོ་རོ་དོན་ཆེན་བསྐྱབས་པར་ཤོག །

སེང་གེའི་དེ་རོ་འཁོར་བ་སྟོང་ནས་དཀྲུགས་པར་ཤོག །

གནས་རིགས་པ་སྤྲུན་རས་གཟིགས་ཀྱི་གདུན་ས་ཟ་ར་ས་སོ། །

འཁོར་རེས་པ་ཡོ་གི་ཆུ་གངར་བ། །

དུས་རེས་པ ༢༠༠༢ ཟླ་བ ༩ ཆོས ༢༢

ཆོས་རེས་པ་སྤྲུན་རས་གཟིགས་བསྐུན་འཆོན་རྒྱ་མཆོ། །

བཅུན་ས་རིག་འཆོན་ཆོས་བཟང་ནས། །

རྩྱ་འཇོན་ཁྱབ་བཟང

So that all beings may attain Awakening
I take refuge in the three jewels found in the deepest reaches
of the heart.

NAMO PUDZA HO BENZA SATO AH

I am delighted by virtues.
I pray that you turn the wheel of dharma,
And that you remain in this world,
That I may be able to perform suitable conduct,
perfect and good.
I beseech you, Amithaba, the changeless reality,
Chenrezi, the joyous body of boundless compassion,
The great pandit of Oddiyana, born miraculously,
Drive away all illness, harmful influences, and obstacles.
When the final malady occurs at the moment of death,
May I escape suffering
And be purified of illusion as this life declines.
May I be reborn on Potala Mountain
In the paradise of happiness,
Or on the glorious Copper Mountain.

Om ame dewa hri
Om mani peme hung hri
Om ah hung benza guru pema siddhi hung

May the lion's roar be everlasting,
May the lion's roar shake samsara at its very foundation,
May the lion's roar be a great benefit for all beings.
May the lion's roar accomplish an ocean of beneficence in
teachings and in beings

The perfect location is the seat of Tchenrezi, Dharamsala,
The perfect company is the yogi of waterfalls,
The perfect time is the 21st day of the 8th month of 2001,
The perfect teaching is that of Tenzin Gyamtso The true Tchenrezi.

THE VENERABLE RIGDZIN TCHEUZANG

CONTENTS

FOREWORD BY LAMA TRA   xiii

INTRODUCTION   1

PART ONE

The Origin and History of Sengueï Ngaro

1   THE LION'S ROAR   6

2   THE UNINTERRUPTED LINEAGE OF SENGUEÏ NGARO   16
Lama Daidot • The Nine Generations • Lama Bui • Yogi Tchouzar Pa

PART TWO

The Philosophy of Sengueï Ngaro

3   WHAT MUST BE REJECTED   36

4   WHAT MUST BE ADOPTED   45
The Four Immeasurables • The Six Transcendent Perfections • The Wisdom of Sengueï Ngaro

PART THREE

The Practice of Sengueï Ngaro

5 THE PROFOUND TECHNIQUES OF SENGUEÏ NGARO   98
    The Postures of Standing Meditation
    The Eight Short Movements and the
        Eight Long Movements
    The Form of the Eighty-Six Movements
    The Form of the Forty-Two Palms of the Buddha
    The Song of the Lotus Rosary
    The Form of the Fisherman Lama
    The Form of the Eight Movements That Empty
        and the Eight Movements That Fill

6 THE SECRET TECHNIQUES OF THE ANIMALS   118
    The Wisdom of Dun Dro Tchou
    The Spirit of the Animals
    The Form of the Ten Animals
        The Bear • The Tiger • The Mongoose • The Crane •
        The Crab • The Praying Mantis • The Monkey •
        The Snake • The Butterfly • The Dragon

7 THE ULTIMATE TECHNIQUES OF SENGUEÏ NGARO   129
    The Form of the Five Animals
    The Form of the Ten Circles

PART FOUR

Yoga Tchouzar: The Essence of Sengueï Ngaro

8 THE EXCELLENT TECHNIQUES OF SENGUEÏ NGARO   140
    Tchou and Ksar • The Art of Mixing the Waters •
    Sengueï Ngaro and Meditation

9 THE FOUR ELEMENTS   150
    Water
        The Great Waterfall of Bodhicitta • The Wisdom of Water

Earth
The Refuge Island • Mount Meru •
The Obstacle Mountain • The Inseminating Island
Air
The Cloud of Impermanence • The Cloud of the Law •
The Anointing of the Bodhisattvas
Fire
Meri Barwa: The Fire Peak • The Wisdom of Fire •
The Seven Flames • The Seven Qualities of the Fire of Tummo

PART FIVE

The Kingdom of Shambhala

10 SENGUEÏ NGARO AND SHAMBHALA   168
The Eight Provinces • The Five Elements •
Kalachakra and Shambhala • The Rigden Kings

11 LING GESAR   176

12 THE ADAMANTINE SWORD   181
The Sword of Wisdom • The Sword of the Bodhisattva

CONCLUSION   187

THE ELEVEN VESSELS OF NECTAR   189

ACKNOWLEDGMENTS   191

GLOSSARY   192

ABOUT THE COLOR ILLUSTRATIONS   195

NOTES   200

ABOUT THE AUTHOR   202

INDEX   203

FOREWORD

For many years and with the greatest secrecy, my teacher, Lama Bui, transmitted to me the Tibetan martial art called Sengueï Ngaro. When we parted, he advised me as follows: "Take good care of your health and always continue your training!" Now at the age of sixty, I am still following this advice as best I can.

He also made me especially promise to transmit this teaching as a whole to an individual with the physical and spiritual ability to preserve it in a state of untarnished purity.

Through my pupil and friend, Yogi Tchouzar Pa, I have been able to keep my promise. And more than that, through this book he has found a way to make the wisdom of the lama warriors known, so that all may benefit.

I hope that Sengueï Ngaro will very soon be practiced by everyone, young and old alike, since it touches what is innermost in us all.

LAMA TRA,
SENGUEÏ NGARO MASTER AND
TEACHER OF YOGI TCHOUZAR PA

INTRODUCTION

The sacred dharma that can't be expressed in words or
thoughts,
Even if you were not to practice it with nonaction and
detachment,
At the very least, may you vow not to consider it as a
definition conceived for the intellect.

DRUKPA KUNLEY

Sengueï Ngaro is a traditional martial art dating back at least to the fifteenth century, in the Kham district of eastern Tibet. Originally conveyed in the greatest secrecy to a small number of disciples, sometimes to a single individual, its oral instructions have been transmitted, without interruption, by a lineage of Tibetan lama warriors. The lama warriors practiced these techniques daily, and always associated them with meditation and contemplation.

Beginning with its founder, Lama Daidot, the teaching has been handed down through eight generations to my teacher, Lama Tra, who is now sixty years old. Now Sengueï Ngaro will be revealed here almost in its entirety, that all may benefit.

Although Sengueï Ngaro is essentially a martial art, it is intended for all who wish to profit from the teachings. Its techniques of bodily defense, combined with advanced meditation on the ultimate nature of spirituality and phenomena, are elements of a progressive training that may extend over several years. Sengueï Ngaro also includes a philosophy that is specific to the Tibetan cultural tradition: the philosophy of the "warrior of Awakening," which is derived from the living wisdom of the Tibetan lamas.

Passed on from teacher to student, the practice, the teaching, and the commentaries of Sengueï Ngaro usually include several levels suited to the capabilities of each individual. In this book we are able to give only an approach to them. Therefore, it is up to every sincere and motivated seeker to follow this path accompanied by a teacher. In fact, without a qualified guide, it is easy to become lost on the martial arts path and confuse results with the ultimate aim: Awakening.

In former times, the masters of Sengueï Ngaro particularly stressed the extreme importance in the manner of listening to and expounding upon instruction. My master, Lama Tra, always reiterated, "Look into your mind. You need to study the deep meaning of what I'm going to teach you today, so you can discard the three incorrect attitudes and delve into the practice of virtue."

There are pitfalls in the teachings that are going to be brought to light in this book. Some who read these instructions may not have their attention directed toward the teaching; they will be like an overturned pot. Others may well read them with attention, but if their motivation is incorrect, their insight will be faulty; they will be like a pot that is upright, but is dirty. And it may be that still others who read this material will grasp neither the words nor their meaning, possibly even forgetting them or distorting their sense, so that their reading won't be of much use to them; such readers will be like a leaky pot.

The Buddha himself cautioned, "Listen to the teaching with good motivation and firm attention, and remember it."

His Holiness the Seventeenth Gyalwang Karmapa and several teachers of the various lineages of Tibetan Buddhism encouraged me to make the art of Sengueï Ngaro known and to share it with everyone.

An integral part of the cultural tradition of Tibet, it is deeply imbued with the dharma teachings, which is why this martial art of the lama warriors cannot really be practiced without knowledge of Tibetan wisdom. Using my experience as a practicing Buddhist, I will attempt to throw light on this unrecognized traditional art so that its essential wisdom can shine through.

My sincere wish is that the essence of Sengueï Ngaro be firmly implanted in everyone's heart, and that it envelops each of you in peace and compassion. I hope this book will lift a corner of the veil on this marvelous and mysterious tradition from Tibet by revealing its bountiful riches—a wealth that is not only historical, artistic, and philosophical, but also spiritual.

PART ONE

The Origin and History of Sengueï Ngaro

CHAPTER ONE

THE LION'S ROAR

SENGUEÏ, THE PROTECTING LIONESS

Sengueï Ngaro is the original name given by Lama Daidot to the martial art that he perfected. Literally, it means "the roaring of the lion." The term *sengueï* designates the snow lioness, a mythical animal, protector of the Himalaya. In the ancient Bön tradition in Tibet, this animal is associated with the tiger, the garuda, and the dragon. In the practice of the five animals called *lung ta*, "wind horse," the snow lioness is associated with a practice that is designed to strengthen internal energy.

These animals—snow lioness, tiger, garuda, and dragon—are very often seen on multicolor prayer flags fluttering in the wind, and were also emblazoned on the victory banners of *khampa** warriors. Sometimes the legendary Ling Gesar, riding a white charger, is featured as a central figure. (See plate 8.)

This same mystic lion is also represented on the base of the tchorten (shrines) in Tibet. This part, called the lion throne, in essence symbolizes superiority over the universe. Traditionally, two lionesses

---

*Khampa warriors are the fierce, skilled, and sometimes unruly warriors from the Kham region of eastern Tibet who protected His Holiness during his 1951 flight from Lhassa.

are portrayed on either side of a flaming triple jewel* or a double *dordjé*.† Sometimes, the snow lioness and the three other animals may each be represented separately on the four sides of the *tchorten,* or even of a temple.‡

The snow lioness is also found in Tibetan painting—in *thangkas,*§ for example—and she can be seen on the present-day national Tibetan flag. Even in the distant past, Tibetan coins were minted with the image of the snow lioness. She dwells in the heart of the tradition, and in a way, she is the protectress of the profound richness this culture represents. One might even say that she is the guardian of the identity of the Tibetan people.

It is clear, then, that there is a very deep connection between the symbol of the lion—king of the animals—and the gift of protection, which is one of the virtues cultivated by the practitioner of Sengueï Ngaro. (See "The Gift of Protection," in chapter 4.)

The martial art of Sengueï Ngaro is symbolized by a roaring lion. Just as the lion protects the clan by keeping guard against approaching danger and wild animal attacks, the practitioner of Sengueï Ngaro conveys protection to all those around him. This protection must be natural, spontaneous, and above all boundless, because the snow lioness is not an ordinary lioness. Her protection is not limited to those beings in her care; it extends to all living beings.

NGARO, THE ROAR OF TRUTH

The word *sengué* is associated with the strength of the lion and with valiant martial courage, whereas the term *ngaro,* meaning "roar" or

---

Triratna in Sanskrit, symbol of the Buddha, the dharma, and the *sangha,* or spiritual community.

†*Visvavajra* in Sanskrit, symbol of indestructibility.

‡These four animals can be found on the exterior of the temple built by the Sixteenth Gyalwang Karmapa in Kibi, India.

§*Thangkas* are traditional Buddhist banners usually hung on altars or carried by monks in ceremonial processions.

"roaring," is associated with truth or *dharma* (proper conduct), and with the spiritual and artistic dimension of Sengueï Ngaro.

This comes from the fact that in the teachings of the Buddha, the truth is compared to the roaring of the lion who awakens the six classes of beings from underlying ignorance, from inertia, and from hatred. (See "Air," in chapter 9.)

The Buddha himself was proclaimed Shakya Sengué—the lion of Shakya, Shakya being the clan to which he belonged.

According to the history of the life of the Buddha Shakyamuni, Ashita, having visited the child Buddha, saw that the gods were rejoicing that a *bodhisattva** had been born in the palace of King Suddhodana. Based on marks on the child's body, Ashita prophesied that the child would become a Buddha. The gods announced to Ashita, "He who is supreme among beings, the preeminent man, like a powerful, roaring lion, the king of the beasts, it is he who will make the wheel of dharma turn in the grooves of Isipatana."

Following this, Ashita visited the king and was able to see these marks for himself. His heart overflowing with joy and faith, he then exclaimed, "He is peerless among the most enlightened of human beings!"

This attribution of the title of Roaring Lion to the Buddha recurs in certain texts where he is proclaimed as the leader who roars his lion's roar in the assemblies. This metaphor designates the particular assurance of the Buddha, who remains in a state of complete calm. The Sixth and Eleventh Buddha of this *kalpa*† will be called Sengueï Ngaro. They, too, will perform their activities in order to establish a foundation for beings in the sublime spirit of Awakening.

It is also predicted that the Sixth, as well as the Eleventh Buddha, will bear the name Sengueï Ngaro, the "Lion's Roar." It was foreseen they will be, respectively, the emanations of the great lamas Gyalwang

---

*One who is predestined.
†The duration of Brahma's day; a cosmic cycle; a very long period of time.

Karmapa and Djé Tsongkhapa. This symbolizes their bravery while revealing their teachings, but also symbolized the secret link that connects the "Buddha Lions," particularly the Fourth, Eleventh, and Hundredth Buddha (Sakyamuni Buddha, Sengueï Ngaro Buddha, and Mospatouk Buddha), with the art of the Lion's "Roar."

Fearless like the lion, they remain intrepid and serene, never fearing to face any obstacle that rises up before them on the path of Awakening.

According to the teaching delivered by Sengueï Ngaro, "When one attempts to follow this martial way linked to the lama warriors' wisdom, progress may become rewarding only through practice, study, and reflection." Then Sengueï Ngaro will be revealed from many different angles that might be illustrated and noted—for *ngaro* means the "roaring" of truth—but the state of a lion can be achieved only through unremitting practice, since *sengueï* means "the Snow Lioness." Then only the "lion's roar" will act for every being's good, and reveal its whole sense and richness. Therefore Sengueï Ngaro may be defined in various ways: the lion's roar, a personal philosophy, a Buddhist practice, a Tibetan martial path within the traditional martial arts, a way of life leading to peace and compassion against each kind of aggression, a secret martial dance comprising more than eighty forms (classified into four domains: peace, expansion, power, and submission), a martial technique based on the protection of life (contrary to every other martial art), a body of knowledge tinged with all the beauty and richness of Tibetan Buddhist art, a secret yoga technique (like Yoga Tchouzar) practiced within the elements linked to the mystical Tibetan ascetics, the knightly way (linked to this worldly century) of the Rigden warriors of the legendary kingdom of Shambhala, and a martial discipline unfolding among a code of ethics (the Eleven Vessels of Nectar), which is intended to improve the spirit of Awakening for every being's good.

ADAMANTINE, DIAMOND-LIKE WRATH

The roaring of the lion, through an action always arising from *bodhi,* or enlightenment, allows the three poisons of the mind to be vanquished. Lama Tra often said to me, "Act with courage and strength. Act from your instruction and from clarity!"

The strength of the lion is that of truth, which, like a perfect mirror, sends negativity back to its source. To conquer negativity, an adamantine wrath is required: the *vajra* anger.

It follows, then, that when a practitioner of Sengueï Ngaro has to intervene to help a person in danger, when he is practicing a martial form for his own training, or when he is showing certain elements to a student, he must, in such situations, remain in the meditative absorption of the indestructible vajra that is called adamantine wrath.

In order to remain in the state of vajra pride, he must realize that all sounds, perceptions, and thoughts are indistinguishable from his vajra nature. This adamantine wrath is splendidly represented in Tibetan Buddhist iconography, in the paintings or sculptures of the male or female wrathful deities called "protectors" or "protectresses" of the dharma.

In the teachings of Sengueï Ngaro it is said that this adamantine wrath, or vajra anger, has multiple qualities. Its essence has been described perfectly by the bodhisattva Tchana Dordjé. (See plate 14.)

As a result of this adamantine wrath, all negative karma in beings is annihilated. All those who are in conflict with others, and who find themselves in pain and suffering, will be delivered from it.

Many other virtues are also attributed to it: invulnerability, indestructibility, truth, solidity, resoluteness, invincibility, providing attainment to those who lack it, making attainment irreversible in those who already have it, transfixing and astonishing all beings.

If you want to imagine this kind of wrath, you need only close your eyes and imagine the stupendous roaring of a lion a few inches away from you!

THREATENING DORDJÉ AND MUDRA

This symbolism of adamantine wrath is found in the Tibetan iconography of fearsome deities: the *dharmapalas*. Just as a dharmapala was said to protect the doors of the *mandala* and the central divinity, the practitioners of Sengueï Ngaro protected a temple and the highest-ranking lamas, called "rinpoches," or "precious ones."

This symbolism, which combines wisdom and martial arts, is found in certain iconographies of the protector deities called *pawo* or *khandro*, in Tibetan and in Vajrayana Buddhism. Certain among them are even associated directly with the snow lioness. Surrounded by flames of wisdom, protectors such as Tchana Dordjé, "he who brandishes the dordjé," and Sengué Dradrok, "the roaring lion," are examples of this kind of protecting divinity animated by adamantine wrath. Colored dark blue like the midnight sky and of very wrathful aspect, they dance brandishing the dordjé—symbol of adamantine wisdom—in the right hand, while with the left hand they make a menacing gesture. This gesture of a pointing finger threatening beings animated with negativity is also used in certain martial arts forms of Sengueï Ngaro.

Last, the symbol of the snow lioness is found in the representation of various peaceful or wrathful deities, such as Djampel Yang (see plate 6), Dhamchen Dordjé Lekpa, Nechung Dordjé Drakden (see plate 11), and Tashi Tseringma,* who serves as their steed. Sengué Dradrok wears the skin of the snow lioness across his shoulders, and it is a useful symbol for identifying him. This aspect of Padmasambhava, the great yogi of Oddiyana, represents the moment when he took the wrathful form to proclaim the truth of the dharma as a roaring lion. He is clothed in a lion's skin because this attribute of the great master links him to a lion.

---

*Principal protectress of the Kagyupa lineage of Tibetan Buddhism, who brandishes a dordjé and a *bumpa,* a vase topped with a flaming jewel. In the time of the great yogi Milarepa, this divinity lived on the mountain of Chomolhari.

THE LION'S LAMAS

Throughout the Tibetan vajrayana tradition, praise and homage are rendered to the great lamas of the past who, roaring like lions, proclaimed the essential teachings.

This comparison between the lama and the lion can be found, for example, in the song of the famous yogi Drukpa Kunley, as he offers up praise to the five great precious founding saints of the Sakyapa lineage:

> *Destroying the game animals of heretical*
>   *opponents,*
> *Inhabiting a mountain of emptiness,*
> *Bearing a mane of the five bodies,*
> *You are utterly majestic,*
> *You, who are called the lions,*
> *I salute you.*

According to the oral tradition of Sengueï Ngaro, one day after an intensive session of his art, Lama Daidot felt his body, legs, and voice become those of a lion. This version of the story, which approaches legend, would seem to signify that his strength and wisdom had attained their pinnacle, and that his practice was perfectly interpenetrated with the deep teachings of dharma.

The term Sengueï Ngaro has appeared elsewhere. There is a text from the Nyingmapa *terton** Jigme Lingpa called *The Roaring of the Lion*, or *Sengueï Ngaro*. However, in the Tibetan martial arts tradition that carries this name, the expression Sengueï Ngaro essentially designates the art practiced by the lama warriors who embodied this teaching in its entirety, and who brought it into existence.

---

*A *terton* is the discoverer of a hidden treasure text (*terma*).

THE LAMA WARRIORS

There were very few lama warriors, or *dragpo lamas,* in Tibet. Only a few individuals bore this secret title as a result of their practice of Sengueï Ngaro. This practice was part of a series of four activities, and centered on one called *dragpo,* meaning "violent subjugation."

The four types of activity practiced by the masters of Sengueï Ngaro are designed to help people eliminate circumstances that are contrary to the dharma. The first is the activity of pacification, or *zhiba.* The second is that of development, or growth, and is called *rgyas pa.* The third is mastery, or *dbang,* and the fourth concerns the activity of violent sub-jugation, or dragpo.

Since Sengueï Ngaro falls into the category of the fourth type of activity, the lamas who engaged in exercise in order to dissipate aggres-sion through the practice of an art that was essentially martial were called lama warriors, or dragpo lamas. In fact, there is a wrathful aspect of the great pandit of Oddiyana, Guru Rinpoche, which is called Dordjé Dragpo—"the adamantine wrathful one," which designates the awak-ened aspect he assumed when he subjugated forces that were hostile to the propagation of Buddhism in Tibet.

The expression "dragpo lama" also has a connection with the origin of Sengueï Ngaro and the legendary kingdom of Shambhala. Specifically, this connection is with the last king of Shambhala, named Dragpo Khorlo in the Tibetan tradition, meaning "the wrathful one of the wheel." He is often portrayed in a martial aspect, riding a white charger and piercing his enemy with a lance. Dragpo Khorlo also exer-cised the wrathful activity of dragpo lama in being represented in the aspect of a protector of Buddhist doctrine, and spreading widely the doctrine of the *kalachakra,* or wheel of time. (See chapter 10, Sengueï Ngaro and Shambhala.)

The ancient Tibetan expression of "lama warrior" needs to be clari-fied. It does not mean soldier monks, or even lamas who have chosen a warpath rather than a spiritual one. Instead, it refers to truly realized beings who put Buddhist philosophy and wisdom into practice in their daily lives and in all their activities. Of course, having great compassion is not enough when one is confronted with aggression and has no means to overcome it, so the lama warriors developed various skillful means designed to conquer aggression, regardless of the form it might take. This could manifest in a number of negative provocations that are sensed to come from beings other than humans.

In the teachings of Senguëi Ngaro, it is explained that one can have recourse to certain specific practices if the provocation or situation of conflict arises from classes of powerful beings. According to the Buddhist teachings of the ancient Bön tradition, these negativities, which are also described in Tibetan medicine, have been categorized into eight classes of beings. Here there is a commonality between Senguëi Ngaro and the Buddhist traditions of Tibet.

According to Gyalwang Namkhaï Norbu, the *mamos,* for example, are at the origin of wars, disputes, and certain kinds of conflicts. There is also a class called *gyalpo,* a kind of evil spirit, which is behind much physical aggression and situations of conflict among beings. Gyalwang Namkhaï Norbu himself received from his uncle, who was a Dzogchen master, the transmission of a practice called *guru drapo kilaya,* or *guru dragpur.* This practice allows all types of disturbances arising from the eight classes to be controlled.

The term *dragpo* is also associated with this kind of practice, as in *dordjé dragpo kilaya,* or also *dragpur.**

According to Gyalwang Namkhaï Norbu, although certain of these gyalpos may have been honored as guardians of particular schools, creating a connection with them is not recommended. As he states, this is because you must "be a master like Padmasambhava if you want to con-

---

Dragpur is a wrathful manifestation represented in the form of a wrathful deity. Its lower body is in the shape of a *purba* (triple-bladed dagger). This information comes from a terma, that is, a text hidden by Padmasambhava. This protector brandishes a scorpion in his left hand. The scorpion is the symbol of total control over gyalpos and all forms of negativity.

trol such powerful beings. Being simply a knowledgeable master is not adequate. These guardians bring more problems than benefits. Because of this, His Holiness the Dalai Lama specifically asked us to no longer practice the gyalpos."

This is why the attitude of a lama warrior must be oriented exclusively toward compassion. Compassion is perfected when one's attitude is directed mainly toward the welfare of others and their release from suffering, whether that is caused by emotion, enemies, or harmful nonhuman entities.

The activity of dragpo, then, is one of a number of paths that foster a benevolent attitude in the spirit of Awakening, eventually leading all beings, without exception, to a state of enlightenment. This is illustrated in the following profound thoughts of the Very Venerable Lama Guendune Rinpoche:

We must preserve the *bodhicitta,* the perfected attitude, which strives to bring enlightenment to all beings including our enemies, negative entities, and those who harm us. We must put into practice immediately all the means at our disposal to help other beings. If we cannot help, we must, just the same, henceforth and forever, merge with bodhicitta.[1]

CHAPTER TWO

THE UNINTERRUPTED LINEAGE OF SENGUEÏ NGARO

ཞེ་བ་གྡོ་ནེ་ངཱ་རོ

THE FOUNDER, LAMA DAIDOT

The history of Sengueï Ngaro is not a legend. It was around the fifteenth century that Tibetan monks found the need to create a defensive technique that was to become a true martial art. This was needed so that they could defend themselves against the harmful acts of the khampas.

These Tibetan bandits, renowned for their art in war and their ferocity in combat, lived in the eastern region of Tibet called Kham. At that time they regularly kidnapped high officials of the monasteries—the rinpoches, or "precious," deeply venerated lamas of high rank—as well as the lamas who were doctors, the *amchis*. Then they exacted enormous ransoms and, once their captives were freed, repeated the same bad deeds all over again.

The first martial art techniques of Sengueï Ngaro began in this climate of constant insecurity. They are still transmitted today as the "profound, secret, ultimate, and excellent techniques of Sengueï Ngaro."*

---

*The techniques originally included only three animals: the crane, *Dja thrung thrung;* the monkey, *Tre ou;* and the praying mantis, *Söl wa dep bu sin.*

The martial art was founded by a Buddhist lama named Ah Dat Ta, also known as Lama Daidot. This first patriarch was born in Tibet in the region of Kham to a family of Tibetan nomads who traveled between Tibet and Qinghai. After he had been ordained as a monk in Tibet, he lived in a temple near Debrung. Eventually Lama Daidot withdrew to the mountains for several years to practice meditation and secret *vajrayana* yoga. One day, while observing the combat of a monkey and a crane, he was inspired to create the first secret animal techniques of Sengueï Ngaro.

The roaring of the lion, Sengueï Ngaro, was the first name given to this martial art. According to the oral tradition, one day Lama Daidot received a transmission directly from the snow lioness as he pointed one finger toward the sky and the other toward the earth. He felt that his hands, his knees, and his voice were those of a lion.

Furthermore, also according to the oral tradition, it seems that many of the secret teachings of Sengueï Ngaro originated with a *togden,* an enlightened, ascetic yogi who lived in a nearby mountain cave. Lama Daidot requested that he provide a teaching adapted to the defense of the monks, while retaining the discipline, ethics, and wisdom promulgated by the Buddhist schools of the Tibetan monasteries.

This martial art was then founded on a system of techniques consisting of eight combinations or postures, eight short strikes of the fist, eight long strikes of the fist, eight strikes with the foot, and so on. Following the lead of Lama Daidot, the monks added this martial art of Sengueï Ngaro to their Buddhist practice.

THE NINE GENERATIONS

After Lama Daidot, the tradition of Sengueï Ngaro was carried on without interruption as a lineage, just like the various schools of Tibetan Buddhism, by the Sengueï Ngaro lama warriors who practiced this art.

With each generation, new techniques were added by the lama warriors of the Sengueï Ngaro lineage. Their secret techniques were inspired by the observation of animals and by the deepening of basic principles of the initial martial forms. At the same time, the profound techniques established by Lama Daidot were preserved, enriching and completing this martial art.

It should be emphasized that all the new techniques added over the course of generations did not dilute the essence of this martial art, but instead have contributed to its richness. Much more than simple additions, these contributions reveal the true and sacred character of Sengueï Ngaro, which, like a mandala,* contains ever-increasing and various potentialities that radiate outward from a primordial and unaltered central core.

A derivative branch of the lineage of Sengueï Ngaro was developed and promulgated in China under the name of Lama Chuan Pai, "the martial school of the lamas." This was to distinguish it from the Chinese tradition of kung fu, the art that was founded in China at the Shaolin monastery by the Tibetan yogi Padampa Sangye, better known under the name Bodhidharma.

At the time of master Hsing Lung, the art of Lama Chuan Pai was modernized and it adopted the name Hop Gar, "the knight's style." However, none of these schools possesses the complete teachings of the original lineage of Sengueï Ngaro, especially its *excellent* and *ultimate* techniques.

In this way, the lineage extended over five hundred years: leaving Tibet and passing through the north of China, then returning to Tibet, finally appearing in Spain, and emerging shortly thereafter in France. So this lineage passed through eight generations to arrive at the present day. I myself am one of the last inheritors of this ancestral Tibetan tradition, having received the teaching of Sengueï Ngaro from my master, Lama Tra, who received it from his master, Lama Bui.

---

*In Tibetan: *kyilkhor,* literally "center" (*kyil*) and "periphery" (*khor*). Sacred geometric representation of the universe in its aspect as a microcosm (for example, a snow crystal) or a macrocosm (for example, the various planets revolving around the sun).

LAMA BUI, THE FLIGHT FROM TIBET

Lama Bui (1900–1981) is the last of the Sengueï Ngaro lamas to have lived in a monastery in Tibet. His parents, who came from Vietnam, entrusted him at a young age to a Tibetan monastery so that he would be educated in the art of Sengueï Ngaro and would study the Buddhist teachings in order to become a lama.

His master gave him the title "Holder of the Lineage of Sengueï Ngaro," once he had learned the whole body of techniques termed "profound, secret, ultimate, and excellent," as well as the technique of the long staff called "fisherman lama," and the "nine secrets" (in Tibetan: *sengueï ngaro sangwa gu*).

Lama Bui unfortunately had to flee from Tibet at the time of the Chinese invasion and the destruction of his master's monastery. This Tibetan monastery was unusual, secretly training lamas in the art of Sengueï Ngaro. Lama Bui had become a master in this art and was invested with the tradition. He had even become the head of the monastery, and being in charge of the teaching, he trained every day.

However, one day his fate hung in the balance. Very early on that particular morning, as custom warranted, he was gathering bat droppings in caves right behind the monastery so that they could be sold to peasants as fertilizer in order to make some money for the monastery. When he heard shouting in the distance, he rushed in the direction of the sound.

Horrified, he discovered that the shouts came from his companions, the monks and lamas, who were being arrested and killed by the Chinese army. His wish to go and help them was great but he knew at the same time that what was most precious, more precious than his own life, was his art and his tradition. Since he carried this treasure within him, he had to survive this massacre. It would have been cowardly to stay hidden in caves, and foolhardy or suicidal to fight against the Chinese.

His attention was suddenly drawn in the direction of the temple garden by the rags of a scarecrow that were flapping in the wind. It then occurred to him that if these dilapidated clothes were able to scare away hungry birds, they would undoubtedly be effective against the Chinese. Making up his mind, he grabbed the old rags, put them on instead of his lama warrior attire, which was much too striking, and set out along the road that led right past the monastery.

As he neared the main gate, he was able to make out, with fear and sadness, the bodies of his Sengueï Ngaro friends and brothers lying in pools of blood. Suddenly, a soldier grabbed him and asked him what he was doing there. Lama Bui immediately responded in Vietnamese. Unable to understand him and seeing that he was decked out in tattered clothing more like a beggar than a lama or warrior monk, the Chinese soldier let him go, urging him to move on and leave the area immediately. Lama Bui didn't hesitate but left, weighed down by the leaden memory of his murdered companions.

Secretly, he returned to Vietnam and then with the help of friends made his way to Spain. He took refuge in the south near Grenada, so that he could preserve his martial art from being lost. He then transmitted in secret the whole of Sengueï Ngaro to his student, Lama Tra.

This is how the tradition of Sengueï Ngaro escaped massacre and oblivion. Lama Bui, now the only holder of this art, chose the just and courageous path in order to safeguard this path and its wisdom, which advocates respect for life. In accomplishing this he showed his true character, that of a Vietnamese hermit who wanted only to follow his calling, enlivened with nonviolence and compassion instead of anger, which would have caused his downfall.

THE TEACHINGS OF LAMA BUI

☯ *Golden Chopsticks*

After my training in Sengueï Ngaro, Lama Tra often told me about certain of his master's teaching that had captured his attention, and which he still remembered.

On the first day of Lama Tra's training in Senguëï Ngaro, Lama Bui invited him to share his meal. Lama Bui accepted and hurried off to look for some place settings that he had carefully taken with him. Near his plate he placed his knife, fork, and spoon.

Lama Bui then asked him, "Would you mind getting a napkin for me?" Happy to be serving his master, he went off, saying, "I'm on my way and I'll be right back."

Upon his return, he noticed that the place settings had disappeared. Stunned, he looked at his master. From behind his back, his master produced two golden chopsticks and gave them to his student saying, "It is forbidden to eat with one's fingers. Here is a pair of priceless chopsticks: One is strength and the other is agility. You must know how to use these two virtues correctly."

Seeing how Lama Bui was eating, Lama Tra tried to imitate him as best he could. Lama Bui had already almost finished his meal and invited his student to do the same.

Unfortunately, after several unsuccessful attempts, he had more rice scattered around his plate than he had managed to get into his mouth. He then exclaimed, "When am I going to be able to feed myself correctly?"

"When you're really hungry, you will manage!" replied Lama Bui, laughing.

Lama Tra's master had just given him a profound teaching in Senguëï Ngaro: knowing how to separate oneself from what is pleasing, and to confront what isn't pleasing. In fact, it is important to ward off irritation and frustration in order to deepen the practice of Senguëï Ngaro, even if they are part of the web of *samara.** Human beings live every day as if seated on a prickly bush, and every time they try to seat themselves more comfortably, they get pricked a bit more. When you meet obstacles, you always need to accept this adversity and find a way to work with people you find aggressive or irritating. Similarly,

---

*The cycle of birth and death.

it's important to be able to separate from what is most loved without suffering for it.

☯ The Iron Ball Wrapped in Silk

Seeing one day that his student was more tense than usual in trying to be strong in his movements, he told him that in the art of Sengueï Ngaro, one must always remember this teaching:

> *The fist is like a ball of steel*
> *Wrapped in a thick layer of silk.*
> *But when the fist arrives at the point of impact,*
> *It's the iron that is felt, not the silk!*

This is a key point in Sengueï Ngaro—the balance between tension and relaxation, and the need to be simultaneously supple and firm. This wisdom is found in the advice of the great yogini Machik Labdrön, who stressed the need to combine flexibility and hardness in the same moment: "Be relaxed and tense at the same time. This is an essential point for your perception."

☯ Punishment with Two Cauldrons

One morning very early, Lama Tra met his master in front of the temple, where he was watching the rising sun. In order to make a happier atmosphere, knowing how much his master liked to laugh and share this expression of energy, he went up to him and after a little while told him a joke. Seeing that Lama Bui remained like a statue, he exclaimed, "So master, this doesn't make you laugh this morning?"

"Today I'm going to punish you with a new training unknown to you," replied his teacher.

Dumbfounded, the student followed. Lama Bui brought his student for the first time into a large hidden room in the temple, where he usually trained alone. There was a strange structure there, a kind of large set of carriage wheels to which were attached two enormous steel cauldrons, one above the other.

"What is that?" Lama Tra asked.

"Your punishment!" replied his master.

He gave Lama Tra two enormous ladles and suggested that his student use them to empty the contents of the lower cauldron into the upper one, which was empty. This was done with a particular rotation of the shoulders based on the mongoose technique. After a short time, the upper cauldron was full. The student, exhausted but pleased with the result, cried out, "I've finished, master!"

At that point Lama Bui turned the huge wheel so that the full upper cauldron was now on the bottom. Then he told his student to repeat the exercise, again and again. This lasted about half an hour.

Once the exercise was finished, he said to his student, "For you, this was a punishment, but for me it is a real pleasure and it makes me laugh a great deal when I do this every morning. I devised and built this wheel for my own training."

Here there is a real martial arts Sengueï Ngaro teaching delivered by Lama Bui to his student. Much more than just a punishment, much more than just a physical, technical training, much more than endurance for his character or his mind developed by this surprising exercise, it is an invaluable lesson. What may appear to some as punishment or suffering can bring a state of calm, fulfillment, happiness, or pleasure to others. The law of karma determines each being's vision of reality.

Its application in the art of Sengueï Ngaro can be explained in the following way. The world of spirit is like an enormous field, and actions in the present are like seeds that are sown. The white seeds of virtuous action bring a future harvest of happinesss, but when black seeds of nonvirtuous action are sown, the harvest is only suffering.

In the Sengueï Ngaro teaching it is noted that these seeds can remain buried in the awareness until their effects have matured. This can take years, several lifetimes even. When you fall asleep with your mind still turning from events experienced during the day, nightmares will arise during sleep. In the same way, an act of aggression may well be the result of nonvirtuous *karma** accumulated in the past or in previous lives. This may help to explain why some people end up fighting, or even killing each other, over a minor dispute.

In Sengueï Ngaro it is said that if you want to protect yourself or protect others from suffering or the risk of aggression, you should avoid creating negative karma in the future, and try to purify the karma that you've already created or accumulated.

Traditionally there are ten primary nonvirtuous actions to be avoided: three connected to the body, four connected to speech, and three connected to the mind.

One of the ten nonvirtuous actions, that of not speaking needlessly, is related to the day that Lama Tra, instead of meditating and respecting the moment of silence when his master contemplated the rising sun, pointlessly told his amusing story. He indulged in useless chatter. The consequence of this kind of speaking, described in the teachings of the Buddha, is that in the future people won't take your words seriously. People will find you stupid and won't pay any attention to what you say, or to your opinions.

Some actions can be considered more harmful than others. Even without pausing to consider whether it is better to use untruthful words instead of words that wound, it's important to understand that harmful is harmful, and that to do nothing against evil is to encourage it.

However, among the ten harmful actions, there are some that are essential to protect against if you want to practice Sengueï Ngaro without deviating from bodhicitta. Crucial nonvirtuous actions are killing (of those relating to the body), speaking hurtful words (of those related to speech), and malevolence (of those relating to the mind). The effects of such actions will very quickly cause you to experience suffering. Conversely, if you develop the opposing virtuous actions—protecting life, using agreeable words with others, and developing benevolence— you will surround yourself with happiness and peace.

---

*The law of cause and effect that carries over through various reincarnations.

Very often, the karmic effects of wickedness and malevolence make someone predisposed to constant fear, and when faced with dangerous situations, panic sets in. In this case, when aggression is encountered, even if he's practicing the secret techniques of Sengueï Ngaro he will not draw any benefit from it or be able to deal with conflict.

Take, for example, someone who is meditating under a tree in a magnificent natural setting, reflecting on the wisdom of equanimity. Suddenly a little red ant bites his leg. He looks down, sees the ant, and immediately crushes it with the back of his hand. He then serenely continues his meditation.

Many people, even after meditating regularly for several years, still have this reflex. If someone is not capable of self-control in the case of such a small gesture, tiny in itself but with incalculable consequences, then taking the life of someone who disturbs him in one way or another would be exactly the same act. Someone who kills an ant can just as well kill a human being the very next day.

It makes no difference whether the object of anger is a simple insect, as tiny as it may be, or a person; anger is present just the same. And if you don't train yourself to protect the life of the tiniest living creature, no matter how disgusting or dangerous it may be, it serves no purpose to practice a martial art such as Sengueï Ngaro, because you would not be applying bodhicitta. And without bodhicitta there is no Sengueï Ngaro! This is a deep and pristine commitment, which practitioners must strive to maintain throughout their lives.

The same holds true if you use cruel words or belittle someone. You then take offense more easily, which leads to more situations of conflict. You can verify this by observation. A wicked person who uses cruel words seems like a snake. As soon as such a person enters a room, he confronts whatever comes his way—his colleagues at work or even the broken coffee machine. Such people create nothing but conflict around themselves.

Conversely, a person with a pleasant demeanor who uses kind words brings a sort of calm, and absorbs situations of conflict with a kind of humor. It is pleasant to encounter such a person, and that person is welcomed everywhere. This also is the art of Sengueï Ngaro.

Many conflicts can be resolved with a smile or a kind word or two, or even the right gesture. Automobile drivers are often antagonistic because kind words and gestures have been replaced by their opposites!

Therefore, to reduce the negative effects of actions, it is important to foster the ten virtuous actions instead of the ten nonvirtuous actions.

It is very difficult to remain calm and untroubled when encountering a situation involving aggression; this is why training in virtuous actions is necessary. It is also necessary to cease committing nonvirtuous actions, and to purify those that have been committed in the past. Certain Sengueï Ngaro teachings show how to practice this purification.

It has been stated that if a person knows the effects of his own past actions but continues to commit them, he is just like a person with perfect eyesight who is about to walk off the edge of a cliff.

The Flame of Wisdom

After some years of training and learning the various martial techniques of Sengueï Ngaro, Lama Tra one day asked Lama Bui, "Master, how is it that I have managed to practice the secret forms of the ten animals more quickly than I could have imagined at the beginning, even though you have not yet taught me the deep meditation of Tibetan Buddhism?"

His master replied, "Some time ago I saw that I had placed a candle in you, and that you had found a way to light its flame."

This teaching illustrates the way that the student's attitude affects his own learning and spiritual progress. Through his generosity, patience, and relaxed ways, Lama Tra had learned, on his own over a period of thirteen years, to live authentically as he spontaneously developed the virtues of the dharma, without deep study of Buddhist teaching.

Lama Tra one day found his master in sequestered meditation. He interrupted him, asking, "Why are you not teaching me more advanced, secret meditation?"

"I'm not a radio station salesman or a door-to-door peddler," Lama Bui laughed gruffly. "Buddhist wisdom is discovered by oneself. Some are born Buddhists, and of those, certain ones will one day discover it."

This relates to his response to a question asked by a student who had completed the entire ten forms of secret techniques: "Don't you find that I've moved rather quickly to have learned all the secret techniques of Sengueï Ngaro?"

"You are perhaps the reincarnation of a lama warrior," his master replied that day.

☯ The Sound of the Bell

One day, Lama Tra came upon his master meditating on the sound of a Tibetan bell held in his left hand. The crystalline sound resounded deeply through the air. Intrigued, he asked him, "Lama, what is the meaning of the sound of the bell that you struck?"

After a long silence, the lama replied, "When the bell is struck, there is the sound that strikes us and represents death; but there is also the sound that continues—unchanged and uninterrupted."

Lama Tra, inspired by his master's metaphor, followed with, "This must be like the continuation of life after death!"

Astonished by the spontaneous response of his student, Lama Bui exclaimed, "You perceive well! You understood and you're not such an idiot as I thought!" And they had a good laugh together.

☯ His Master's Only Praise

As Lama Bui illustrates, it is not usual to flatter or praise the student during the study of Sengueï Ngaro. For a practitioner of martial arts, pride must be banished. One day, as Lama Bui was preparing to attack using techniques called "the crane," he advised his student to counterattack using "praying mantis" techniques. His student correctly improvised lightening responses of great efficiency. Apparently satisfied with the result, the teacher exclaimed, "You see, as animals we get along well!"

This was the first time that Lama Bui had complimented Lama Tra on his practice, and they both began to laugh.

This form of humor, which is very particular to Tibetan lamas, deeply affected Lama Tra during his long apprenticeship. There is a Tibetan saying on this subject:

> *"How does one recognize a real yogi?"* one asks.
> *"By his laugh!"* the other replies.

That doesn't mean that you have to burst out laughing when you encounter a situation of aggression. Laughter would be misplaced if you begin to giggle when someone flings himself at you and wants to beat you with a stick. However, laughter has its virtues, and the difference in behavior and attitude between a person who is jovial and full of humor and a person who is tense and quick-tempered can have consequences for the training of the practitioner. It also can affect how he reacts to an aggressive act or an unusual situation.

One day Lama Tra asked his master, "Why are you always laughing, especially when things are serious?"

To this his master replied, "You're an idiot if you don't know how to laugh! Laughter is healing for your spirit and releases positive energy. Being sullen or angry is just the opposite. Notice how your energy is lost when you take yourself seriously in your training or when you get angry. You feel completely drained."

YOGI TCHOUZAR PA

☉ *The Prediction of Lama Gyamtso*

A dozen years ago, I had the opportunity and good fortune to meet for the first time the *dordjé lopon** of the temple of Kagyu Ling, the venerable Tempa Gyamtso. The venerable lama inquired about my personal

---

*Vajra master: honorific title for a retreat master.

practice, and I confided in him that I had been practicing Chinese and Japanese martial arts for some years. Knowing that this venerable lama was a great yogi and an accomplished master, I asked him, "Should I stop my practice of martial arts and devote myself entirely to meditation and the yoga of the Kagyu school?" And I added, "If you think I should do that, then I will completely stop my practice of martial arts right away!"

Lama Tempa looked at me very hard and after a few seconds of intense concentration, he predicted for me in a firm and confident voice, "No. Don't stop your practice of martial arts. You will practice martial arts right up to the most advanced degree, and at that moment you will come back to the dharma!" Intrigued by such a direct and precise response, I immediately wanted to know more. I then asked my question again, but differently, "Should I, then, one day stop my martial arts and practice only the dharma?"

At that, the venerable lama repeated once again the same response: "You will practice martial arts right up to the most advanced degree, and at that moment you will come back to the dharma!"

Thinking that the venerable lama had perhaps misunderstood my question, I asked the same question a third time, since I still wanted to know more about this strange prediction. "How will I know that I have attained this final stage in the practice of martial arts, and why must I then come back to the dharma?"

Upon hearing this new question, the master smiled and then calmly gave once again this same reply, which remained very puzzling for me: "You will practice martial arts right up to the most advanced degree, and at that moment you will come back to the dharma!"

Understanding that this precise reply of the Venerable Lama Tempa Gyamtso would have meaning only when I had accomplished what he had just predicted for me, I thanked him warmly and took my leave, carrying with me this prediction that affected my future both as a practitioner of martial arts and as a seeker of Buddhist wisdom.

Time passed and it was ten years before I once again met the

Venerable Lama Tempa Gyamtso. Since I had in the meantime received the transmission of Sengueï Ngaro, founded mainly on dharma values such as compassion and transcendent perfection, the predicted cycle was complete. He was delighted to learn that his prediction of ten years prior had been fulfilled.

Being himself from the region of Kham, where he lived before the Chinese invasion, the Venerable Lama Tempa inquired about this martial art, which was unfamiliar to him. He invited me to give a demonstration of Sengueï Ngaro at Plaige (France) in the Temple of the Thousand Buddhas so that he could discover the principles of this discipline that had a strange connection with what he had predicted ten years before.

This was how it came about that in July of the year 2000, the first demonstration in the West of this lama warrior martial art—an art until then transmitted in the greatest secrecy—took place before about sixty people invited by the Venerable Lama Tempa Gyamtso.

At the end of this demonstration, which ended very late at night, the venerable lama made a short commentary on what he had seen, heard, and understood. He strongly recommended this practice, and he encouraged me to teach the art of Sengueï Ngaro to all persons, of any age, so that great benefits would follow.

This is how the prediction of the Venerable Lama Tempe Gyamtso about me was finally brought to fruition.

The Meeting with the Venerable Rigdzin Tcheuzang

A few years later, a meeting with one of the high-ranking female practitioners of the Tibetan tradition of Chö greatly influenced my spiritual path in the art of Sengueï Ngaro.

It was during a trip to Dharamsala that I met the Venerable Rigdzin Tcheuzang, the last holder of the lineage of Chö, which had been founded by the famous woman practitioner Machik Labdrön. She was living in a tiny house deep in a forest above Dharamsala, a place that was inhabited primarily by monkeys of the mountain groves.

When I arrived at the place of her retreat, the venerable lady opened the door and examined me for a long time with a profound gaze, her eyes radiating peace and wisdom. She invited me to come in and to share, as custom required, some Tibetan tea that she had just prepared. She was not surprised by my visit, and immediately told me how happy she was to have found on her doorstep a Westerner who radiated calm and compassion.

My Tibetan friend Sönam,* who accompanied me, then presented me to the Venerable Rigdzin Tcheuzang and explained the difficulties I faced in preserving the art of Sengueï Ngaro, especially since I was the last holder of this lineage. He stressed that I wished to transmit this teaching to future generations.

I summarized for her the extraordinary history of this uninterrupted tradition of lama warriors, and the special nature of this traditional teaching, and I explained its profound philosophy. The venerable lady, with tears in her eyes, was delighted to learn that this art had survived the Chinese invasion. She told me in detail how she herself had been forced to flee Tibet and take refuge in Dharamsala, and recounted all the material difficulties she was facing in order to provide for the needs of all of the nuns housed in her monastery.

Spontaneously, she showed me a photo of her master, the last initiate before her in her lineage. Like a precious relic, this photo was kept in a tiny, two-inch-square frame wrapped in a little clear plastic to protect it from dampness. In this photo I contemplated the face of a woman whose features resembled those of Alexandra David-Néel; her gentle face radiated peace and calm.

Venerable Rigdzin Tcheuzang then kindly suggested writing down specific requests in order to protect the lineage of Sengueï Ngaro and to set forth the richness of this teaching, of which I was the last practitioner. The venerable lady added that she would compose a song, drawing from three basic texts by Opame, Tchenrezi, and Guru Rinpoche in

---

*Longtime friend of the Venerable Rigdzin Tcheuzang. He was mainly working on retranscribing the exceptional biography of this last holder of the lineage of Chö.

order to expound on the essential meaning in the Dzogchen manner. (See plate 7.) In this way, future practitioners would be linked to the path of Awakening. The venerable lady insisted on this, saying, "Senguei Ngaro is not an ordinary art—it allows the attainment of Awakening. You do not need to look for other teachings in the various traditions of Tibetan Buddhism. In fact, if you practice Senguei Ngaro correctly by combining it with this song that I am transmitting to you, you will be placed directly on the path of Awakening. By completing this practice of Senguei Ngaro, you will actually acquire the rainbow body, the *jalu.*"*

We spent very special moments in the company of this great practitioner. There were long discussions on the essential points of Senguei Ngaro and of Dzogchen, notably on contemplation practices using the Tibetan letter *A,* as well as the specific practices of *thögyal,* "moving over the mountain peak." The venerable lady stressed the main points of these contemplation practices and invited me to return the next day to receive the transmission of the text that she was going to compose.

The next day she finished this spontaneous song, which her translator hurriedly transcribed. She made sure the transcription was precise and then gave me the transmission and complete explanation, which lasted almost three hours. She went to some length to stress the importance of this text in ensuring the long life of Senguei Ngaro, threatened as it was with extinction.

She confided in us that she had had auspicious dreams about this Tibetan art and that even if obstacles were to arise, they would be brushed aside. Gazing deeply into the empty space before her for the entire time, she explained word-for-word the deep meaning of what had just been revealed. She asked me to take good care of this text and to transmit it to all those who wanted to practice Senguei Ngaro, commenting, "In the future, many people will practice Senguei Ngaro and

---

*The state of complete mastery wherein the physical body is released at the time of death, leaving behind only nonliving elements like hair and nails.

it is your responsibility not to allow this martial art to become an ordinary art. You will need to be attentive to all the students who follow you, so that they do not stray from the path of wisdom and so that their practice really leads them toward Awakening. If you follow the path of the lama warriors, then you must have no doubt, since this path leads directly to complete enlightenment."

While the venerable lady was giving these explanations, the monkeys fighting on the roof pulled loose the electric wires, and the lights suddenly went out, leaving us in complete darkness. She was not at all upset by this and declared, after lighting a candle, that she was going to continue the transmission. Once she had finished, she encouraged me to promulgate the martial art of Sengueï Ngaro throughout the world, and she promised that she would transmit her wishes in support of this development for the benefit of all.

She offered me a long *khatag,* the traditional white silk scarf, as well as various relics that she prepared for me.

Before leaving, I promised to help her in the reconstruction of her monastery, which was very run-down and where hundreds of completely destitute nuns were living in the most difficult conditions. The venerable lady was very touched by this offer, and willingly accepted.

PART TWO

The Philosophy of Sengueï Ngaro

CHAPTER THREE

WHAT MUST BE REJECTED

BAD CONDUCT

In the martial practice of Sengueï Ngaro, mental attitude is essential. In fact, what makes an act beneficial or harmful is not its appearance or its effect, but the good or bad intention that animates it.

You can want to defend yourself, or lend a hand to someone who is in an aggressive situation, and then not behave in the correct way despite having begun with a good intention. In the heat of action you may make a wrong move, or, worse still, injure the person who has attacked you. You may even kill that person. There is not much benefit in using a martial art based on the preservation of life and the values of the dharma if you end up with the opposite result.

This is why the mental attitude of the spirit of Awakening, bodhicitta, is very important in the martial art of Sengueï Ngaro. It could be said that this is what distinguishes it from other martial arts.

The behavior of the practitioner occupies a very important place in the learning of this martial art. In observing the student, the teacher must be aware that he is distinguishing conduct that must be avoided from conduct that must be adopted.

THE THREE DEFAULTS OF THE CONTAINER

The ethical and martial discipline of Sengueï Ngaro cannot be compared with, for example, the Bushido code of the Japanese samurai. There is nothing in common between refusing to pick a simple flower or to kill the smallest insect and its opposite—calmly chopping off the head of a human being because he simply and unintentionally touched your sword, which is contrary to your code of honor.

In Sengueï Ngaro, respecting life means respecting the tiniest bit around you. You don't need a code for that. It's a natural attitude— either you have it or you don't. The discipline of Sengueï Ngaro speaks specifically of the three defaults and the six stains as being part of what must be rejected.

My master Lama Tra often spoke to me about the three defaults of the container, or the three faulty bowls. The mind of the practitioner is compared to an immaculate container into which the teacher will be able to pour his knowledge and wisdom in such a way that they are not mixed with impurities or allowed to disappear.

Such a container is very rare, and it has happened that certain teachers have been unable to transmit their knowledge to future generations because they could not find a trustworthy and deserving student. The tradition of Sengueï Ngaro almost disappeared several times in the past because of this.

The aptitudes and talents of each person's mind have led to assigning the practitioners to different categories: lower, middle, and higher. Each category is further subdivided into three subcategories: lower lower, middle lower, and upper lower; then lower middle, middle middle, and so on. The different teachings are, in fact, addressed to persons in the three categories according to the capabilities of each individual.

It's not a question of levels, colored sashes, or ranking. If the student, in relation to his physical and spiritual capabilities and his constitution, completes a single teaching, he can then obtain the benefits of all of Sengueï Ngaro. The essential principles of this art are part of each teaching, whether it is addressed to a student with limited capabilities or a student with extensive capabilities. What's important is being able to arrive at the destination. As Lama Tra said, "There's no need for one hundred yaks; one is enough to get you where you're going."

To get there the student must be free of the three defaults and the six stains.

The first default is that of the "overturned container," which symbolizes the situation of not listening to what is being transmitted. Not a single word is heard; not a single movement is seen.

Then there is the "poison-filled container," which symbolizes listening to, or practicing, the teaching with incorrect behavior or a faulty mental attitude. When what is transmitted by the teacher is mixed with the five spiritual poisons—attachment, pride, ignorance, jealousy, and anger—it is of no benefit. Everything that could have been of benefit to the student immediately turns to poison, and his practice will never become authentic and pure.

Last, there is the "leaky container." This means that the student retains nothing of what the teacher has transmitted, not having assimilated the instructions that were given and not having put them into practice. The instructions are useless and a waste of time.

Sengueï Ngaro includes a vast body of teachings and practices. They cannot all be acquired at once or within a short span of time. Some techniques are very physical and often you may be able to do only one or two forms out of twenty. Also, you can practice only a small segment at one time, and then from time to time change and do others.

If you become lax or happen to forget a form, it will be very difficult for you to recall details. This is why it is important to be attentive and watchful when the teaching is being transmitted. It is by remembering direct instructions, often given orally, that we can manage to preserve this tradition unchanged. What's more, no book, no written note, no video recording will be able to safeguard what is transmitted from one mind to another, and is therefore way beyond the form itself. For this to take place you must be free from the six stains; only then can the instructions of Sengueï Ngaro be maintained in a pure and complete manner.

THE SIX STAINS

These apply just as much to the martial techniques as to the practice of meditation.

1. The first is pride, in which you consider yourself superior to the teacher who is transmitting the teaching. It is very difficult to envision the transmission of Sengueï Ngaro in today's world where the value of a teaching, an art, or an instructor is measured by his fame, rank, or the number of his students. His apprenticeship means starting over at zero and putting everything in question: his breathing, the precision of his movements, their exact application in situations of real combat, and, above all, the proper mental attitude.

We might almost speak of a fourth incorrect container: "the too-pricey bowl." You don't have to be a holder of an eighth dan in order to practice Sengueï Ngaro. A four-year-old child can train in a way that is more authentic and continuous than an adult who has twenty years of martial arts training under his belt. The important thing is to get rid of pride, which is a real poison in the path of martial arts.

In Sengueï Ngaro, there is only the student and the teacher. Once the complete teaching has been received—that is, once each movement, each technique has been made part of you—you will have come to the end of what you have learned. You then become a teacher in your own right and can retransmit the totality of your knowledge. There is no intermediary, no competition, no ranking. This is why I think that this martial art derives more from the domain of culture and tradition than from the domain of sport, like kung fu or karate, or certainly from the domain of competition.

2. The second stain is lack of confidence in the teacher and his instruction. This is very important because when you come to the "excellent techniques" of Sengueï Ngaro, where you begin to practice yoga using the elements (earth, air, fire, and water), you need to have real confidence in the teacher and his instruction. A meditation under a winter waterfall would be more than just dangerous if the practitioner decided to do the opposite of what needs to be done. He would risk certain death, just as if when facing an aggressor, he tried to carry out a parry that was the opposite of what was required.

The martial path is much too serious for anyone to deviate by a hair's breadth from the instructions of past teachers, since the knowledge of these masters is based on their deep wisdom and their personal experience of Sengueï Ngaro. This is why it is necessary to have unshakable confidence in the teacher and his instruction.

3. The third stain is the lack of effort in one's practice. Without effort, no positive result can be expected. When faced with difficulties, you may sit back and tell yourself, "I'm stopping here and that will be enough for today," "I'll finish tomorrow," or "I'll do better next time," This is incorrect behavior. In the *Precious Rosary of the Warrior of Awakening,** it is stated:

> *When you start something,*
> *Finish it.*
> *Always act this way,*
> *Otherwise you will accomplish nothing.*

You might very well be overflowing with energy, but it is when your endurance is called upon that your determination will be measured.

---

*Text composed by the Indian Pandit Atisha Dipamkara Shrijnana. See *Conseil d'un Ami Spiritual,* published by the Institut Vajra Yogini, France. Wisdom Publications publishes the English version from which the French was translated: *Advice from a Spiritual Friend.*

Energy can fluctuate: one day you have too much and the next day you don't have enough, or have none at all.

Neither too much nor too little! Using the example of a wood fire, if the fire is too strong, there soon will be no wood left. Conversely, if you don't tend the fire, it will go out and the wood will no longer burn. Right effort is a balance between tension and relaxation.

4. The fourth stain is distraction of the mind by objects outside the six senses.

Certainly, the whistling sword blade or the sight of a hulk attacking can be vital information coming from one of the six senses, allowing an appropriate defense to be mounted. But what is meant here is not falling into distraction: avoiding being caught by passing inclinations or emotion-laden thoughts of the future, or letting present thoughts be distracted by adverse or pleasant circumstances and the objects of the six senses.

The intention is basically not to be distracted by the objects of the six senses, because consciousness can be subject to error, deception, and illusion. The teachings of Sengueï Ngaro speak of the hallucinations of samsara,* which arise from this distracted consciousness that is the source of all suffering.

Pondering that the undetermined hour of death is often caused by this distracted consciousness, a practitioner of martial arts ought to be more afraid of his distracted consciousness than of his bravest opponent.

When the butterfly clings to his visual consciousness of forms, he dies in the candle flame; when the honeybee clings to his olfactory consciousness, he dies before being able to drink the nectar of the carnivorous flower; when the stag lets himself be seduced by the sound of music, he is killed by the hunter; when the elephant craves the coolness of water, he drowns in the mud; when the fish is seduced by the taste of the worm, he dies on the hook. The masters of the past have left us

---

*The cycle of death and rebirth engendered by unresolved karma.

these examples to explain the way in which consciousness is distracted by the six senses.

When faced with adversity, the practitioner must be very watchful and composed. He must not let himself be ambushed by the illusion of what he sees, hears, smells, or touches.

Most of these teachings have a martial arts application, and there are several relating to nondistraction. Certain of them are addressed to the beginning practitioner who must not let himself be distracted by new teachings or become attached to forms, to power, and so on. Others are concerned with the excellent techniques of Yoga Tchouzar and with the "ultimate techniques." Certain practices are carried out, for example, with the eyes blindfolded so that one is not deceived by external forms. This could be said to be one of the ultimate applications of nondistraction in martial arts practice.

Numerous benefits can be drawn from nondistraction. Imagine that certain masters have the ability to move objects at a distance, even huge ones, simply by concentrating their minds. You see, it may be that the unknown assailant you think is behind that bush that just moved is actually lying in wait for you somewhere else—above you, beside you, or behind you!

It is especially difficult to realize that what you take to be real may simply be an illusion, hoax, or trap. And, as in the examples of the animals that were prisoners of their own senses, a distraction can lead to certain death. This is particularly true when someone in front of or behind you, such as a hunter or fisherman, shows up ready to take your life.

The importance of nondistraction isn't limited only to those cases where the opponent has supernormal powers—something rather rare in this day and age. The opponent is often hiding where we don't expect him to be. Like a microbe or a wild animal, he's often crouching in the dark; when he appears, it's already too late to fight. You may very well encounter aggression from different levels.

Someone may pass himself off as another person. This art of a disguise or ruse was frequently used in certain medieval schools in Japan.

It can also be the case of someone quite charming, a friend, for example, who later turns out to be an enemy. You don't expect this—it's like the carnivorous plant, or the hook that is hidden by the worm. There's a Tibetan image of a knife covered in honey. You lick the honey, it's very pleasant, but it's immediately followed by pain and suffering. Something that's a source of pleasure can very quickly turn into suffering. This is the law of impermanence.

It's also possible for this to arise in oneself. Human beings never mistrust themselves enough. It's very easy to stray from the path of wisdom and become a monster using one's art to harm others, or to become the greatest—a champion. If you don't cultivate nondistraction, and above all love and compassion, you will very quickly end up with conflict or with war. Like a poisonous snake, the symbol of anger in Tibetan Buddhism, the tendency is to rise up against the first thing that moves. I invite you to contemplate these verses of Thogme Zangpo, in the *Thirty-Seven Bodhisattva Practices:*

> *So long as the inner enemy is not conquered*
> *The outer enemies will continue to increase.*
> *The son of conquerors disciplines his own mind*
> *With the armies of love and compassion.*

5. The fifth stain is self-absorption. To progress in Sengueï Ngaro, self-absorption is just as much an obstacle to understanding the meaning of a teaching as it is to the application of this understanding. This lack of openness cuts the student off from the external environment and prevents him from receiving and putting into practice the teacher's advice and instruction.

6. Discouragement is the sixth kind of stain. Whether this is under duress or just facing the many long years of practice necessary to master this art, the student can very quickly become discouraged. Mastering the knowledge of Sengueï Ngaro often takes an entire lifetime.

As His Holiness Kalu Rinpoche recommended one day to his disciples, "Authentic practice is like a drop of water that runs off a leaf every day and digs into the earth until there's nothing left but rock. If we practice passionately every day and then relax for a certain time, the hole fills in again and all the work has to be redone."

That's the trap of relaxing.

CHAPTER FOUR

WHAT MUST BE ADOPTED

THE PRACTICE OF EXCHANGE

Changing an aggressive situation into one of calm depends entirely on your sympathetic attitude and your intention. In order to bring about this attitude, you must develop a capacity for seeing others as more important than yourself.

This attitude of goodwill and openness allows for awareness of the enemy and for thinking of him with compassion. Lama Tra often said to me, "Compassion is the great strength of the practitioner of Sengueï Ngaro, because it is the source of nonaggression and gentleness."

If you consider your enemy to be more important than yourself, you can turn the aggressive situation around. Being able to do this depends on the strength of your compassion. If your compassion is real and you are more concerned with the well-being of others than with your own, you will be capable of carrying out what is called "the exchange of one-self for another."

This practice, which is called *tonglen* in Tibetan, allows you to con-duct yourself in a nonaggressive manner while developing compassion. *Tong* means "giving" and *Len* means "taking," so *tonglen* literally means "giving and taking." It means taking on the suffering and aggressiveness of others and offering them peace and happiness in exchange.

The practice of exchange leads to the elimination of all struggle and conflict, because it dissolves the barrier that people usually erect between themselves and others. An enemy allows you to increase your good qualities. When you don't respond to his anger, he assists you in the development of nonaggression and the elimination of hatred.

In acting as a lama warrior, one considers whoever manifests aggression and anger as being more important than one's own body. In *The Thirty-Seven Bodhisattva Practices,* which is an essential text for developing the training of the spirit of Awakening in the Tibetan Buddhist tradition, it is stated this way:

> *For a bodhisattva who aspires to the riches of virtue,*
> *Any aggressor is like a precious treasure.*

It is certainly difficult to consider your aggressor as a precious treasure. But it is fundamental to training in bodhicitta, and it is the heart of the practice of exchange. This works not only for anger but also for all other emotions: pride, jealousy, and attachment. So if you come to consider a piece of gold like an ordinary pebble or an ordinary pebble like a piece of gold, then you are perfecting the practice of exchange. Your enemy can become your best friend.

Considered in its martial arts form, Sengueï Ngaro a practice that is influenced in a certain way by the practice of exchange. Meditation in action is an activity of bodhicitta, since it is rooted in compassion and in the will to transform a situation of conflict into one of peace.

When faced with an aggressive situation that demands a reaction, it is first of all vital to have self-confidence and not to feel weak, off-guard, disconcerted, or even threatened by the aggressor. Rather, make use of this precious energy coming from the other person in order to reestablish a situation of nonconflict, peace, and calm.

First of all, put yourself in the place of the other person so that you can perceive the intensity and real tenor of the aggression. In doing this, the situation of conflict can be turned into one of compassion, oriented toward the other person and not centered on yourself. This is a way to really put into practice the attitude that is at the heart of the practice of exchange.

This practice can be considered within the setting of physical aggression from two points of view:

One is the case of a person who is not practicing exchange and the other is when the person is practicing it.

For a person who is not practicing tonglen, the situation is clear: you are faced with an aggressor. You are the object of aggression. The only solution you can find will depend on a number of factors: you can decide to run away or you can decide to fight, in which case you often become the aggressor yourself. In fact, it's difficult to tell who is the aggressor when you see two people fighting. It may be that one hit the other first, but the other one may have insulted the first a few moments earlier.

But the actual cause of the aggression doesn't change the fact that the aggression continues to develop more and more strongly until the two begin to hit each other. Where is legitimate defense really to be found?

In the case of a person who is practicing exchange, even if a conflict situation arises, his practice of tonglen leads him to eliminate all struggle and conflict because this practice rejects the barrier that is usually erected when one is considered to be the aggressor and the other as someone aggrieved. Applying tonglen is not obvious. The first point is certainly difficult: "Take, accept!" How can you accept the unacceptable?

Habitually, we react to aggression and to what displeases us with an attitude of struggle, rejection, or flight. In fact, not responding to insults or not flinching when struck is simply not part of habitual human behavior. It is much more difficult to generate compassion and gratitude toward a person who charges forward, intent on attack, with a weapon in his hand.

This is why the second point is essential: giving. You mustn't misunderstand what this term means. It's not a matter of giving blows, of counterattack, responding to anger with anger, or even of giving up completely. It is not giving up, but giving.

The lama warrior must behave as a bodhisattva and generate the four immeasurables. (See "The Four Immeasurables," page 51.) He gives with compassion, without limit, and without reserve. He gives with a fearless and concentrated attitude, with the courage and confidence of a lion.

In Sengueï Ngaro, training is first of all in the posture of seated meditation and then progresses to meditation in action. If your practice of exchange is forged in the fiery motivation of the spirit of Awakening through assiduous and continual practice, you can really cut through duality in your actions, while at the same time retaining an attitude of openness and compassion.

There are specific meditation exercises in the art of Sengueï Ngaro that allow aggression to be transformed—an attack on one's person, for example—while at the same time enabling an attitude of compassion, during and after the action.

Even if you are hit before you can neutralize the aggression, or realize you have been wounded after having immobilized your aggressor, your action and your breathing remain unaltered as an essential support for the practice of exchange.

EXERCISE WITH THE STAFF

There are exercises specific to Sengueï Ngaro that help you to maintain an attitude of compassion at every moment during the course of a physical aggression.

These exercises are different from one another but are basically related to the practice of exchange and to the subtle relationship among the following: the mind, movement, and breathing. There is a particular one that effectively develops a talent for maintaining compassion while in action, and doing so regardless of the attitude of the aggressor, the methods, the weapons used, or the moment of the aggression, including even the strength, number, or intensity of the blows received.

However, this kind of practice correspondingly aims at developing other capabilities linked to meditation, balance, and the development of energy in movement.

There is a specific exercise in which the student executes a 180-degree downward strike with his staff so that it is carried out for a complete cycle of breathing (in-breath and out-breath). The path of his strike begins behind his back, passes over his head, and ends up in front as if he were cutting an object placed in front of him in two.

The instructor is positioned behind him or to one side so that the student is not affected by blows from the instructor's staff to various specific parts of his body.

The repetition of these blows, the exact spot being hit, their intensity, and even the moment when the blow is delivered will elicit a different response in the student, who must confine himself to carrying out his strike without hitting back and without changing his response. In this way he develops the practice of exchange while in action.

Several experiences may appear in the awareness of the student, and certain extraordinary capabilities can be developed. The student must observe his state at every moment—before, during, and after his movement—and he must continually generate compassion. No aggression or anger must arise, and total confidence, along with unshakable concentration, must be established between the two partners in this exercise.

Through all this the student develops an attitude of openness and calm no matter what takes place. As the tension and the number of blows to his body increase, both the student's calm and his sense of compassion increase as well.

However, this kind of exercise not only helps to develop a relative bodhicitta and exchange but it also helps the student develop absolute bodhicitta and attain emptiness. For that, the student must become aware that there is no launching of the movement, no trajectory in the movement, and no termination of the movement.

In this way he develops perfect movement and nothing can stop his clean strike. His movement is of maximum intensity merged with total concentration. In such moments the student absorbs the oral instructions that have been given, and experiences states of concentration and contemplation specific to the practice of Sengueï Ngaro.

Here is one of the teachings that are part of this exercise. For example, as the student is executing the strike with his staff, the teacher strikes him immediately with his own staff.

The student remains in a state of contemplation for a few seconds after breathing out, and at that moment the instructor may say to him:

> *What seems like movement at the core of stillness,*
> *Disappears at the core of stillness.*
> *What arises as anger at the core of emptiness,*
> *Dissolves at the core of emptiness.*[1]

Of course, it may seem difficult to expect an immediate and spontaneous understanding of these few words and their exact meaning when you have just been given a sharp blow with the staff. A real blow, a physical one! You can still feel the pain exactly where you were hit.

In fact, this has nothing to do with an intellectual or conceptual understanding of bodhicitta, but is simply its practical application during a session of characteristic aggression. And at the moment the student realizes the meaning of what has been stated, he then applies it to his next movement. There is a progression through the exercises and the teachings, but not all the exercises include blows delivered physically.

Let's take the example of oratory jousting between monks. Between each response and after each question, one of the participants claps his hands loudly—not to disconcert or disorient his partner, but in order to create a state free from duality and conceptual seeking. The essential meaning of the response and the clarity of the question are, therefore, spontaneous and immediate. Besides, this gesture of the hands and arms that is carried out during traditional jousting is very close to the gesture of salutation that precedes each session of Sengueï Ngaro.

The real meaning of this kind of teaching is a meditation on the spirit of Awakening in action. If you outline a shape in water with your sword, a trace appears and ripples outward on the surface of the water, and then a moment later, all that is gone. In terms of Dzogchen, this is called self-arising and self-liberation. Of course, this exercise with the staff is closely related to the practice of *trekchö*, letting go, but it is applied in a specific way to the art of Sengueï Ngaro.

This is why the martial arts practices of Sengueï Ngaro can lead equally well to the attainment of relative bodhicitta, or to absolute bodhicitta. In fact, the art of Sengueï Ngaro is really steeped in Tibetan Buddhist wisdom that is linked just as much to Mahayana Buddhism as to Dzogchen.

THE FOUR IMMEASURABLES

It is essential to generate the four immeasurables. In Tibetan, *tshad med bzhi*, they designate the four aspects of the attitude of a bodhisattva who undertakes to guide beings out of suffering: unlimited loving-kindness, unlimited compassion, unlimited joy, and unlimited equanimity. These qualities are termed immeasurable because, since their object is unlimited,* the results and merits arising from this practice are immeasurable.

When speaking of all beings, the reference is to all those in the three times and in all directions. The focus is not only certain beings living in a particular place or moment. This bodhisattva motivation is said to be as limitless as space itself. The unlimited spirit of Awakening embraces all beings in infinite numbers, including your enemies. The four immeasurables are intended to reinforce the spirit of Awakening that has already been developed in the heart of the practitioner.

---

*Their object refers here to an infinite number of beings.

THE SIX TRANSCENDENT PERFECTIONS

In the beginning training involves various meditative practices, in order to develop relative bodhicitta. This consists of creating a benevolent and compassionate attitude. As this attitude develops more and more, it brings out various qualities, such as openness and a warm connection with others.

This training also develops absolute bodhicitta, meaning that the student trains himself to go beyond the illusions that support his grasping at self.

But before attaining this absolute bodhicitta and conquering this dualist grasping, he needs to develop relative bodhicitta, so that it is not just simple aspiration but becomes a real putting into practice in daily life, and in the application of Sengueï Ngaro, regardless of the situation that arises.

Much more than aspiring to move toward the state of being Buddha, in order to be able to help all beings at the subtlest levels, an attitude of compassion toward all those who suffer has to be put into practice. For that, the lama warrior must act as a bodhisattva and cultivate the six perfections: giving, discipline, patience, effort, concentration, and transcendent knowledge.

The practice of the first five perfections leads to the attainment of the sixth perfection: transcendent knowledge. By attaining the perfection of transcendent knowledge, absolute bodhicitta is achieved.

This explains why in the art of Sengueï Ngaro, we strive above all to develop a very precise martial discipline in which it is necessary to cultivate everything that is fundamentally of benefit to beings and to renounce all that is harmful to them.

This martial discipline takes root by practicing the six perfections together. By practicing them we enter the true path of the warrior of Awakening. In this we find the path of courage and fearlessness that belongs to the roaring lion, to Sengueï Ngaro. This path is the path of those who possess the courage of the spirit of Awakening, the bodhisattvas.*

---

*A bodhisattva is one who has the courage of the spirit of Awakening.

☯ The Gift of Protection

When you meet someone,
Take pleasure in giving without avarice.

THE PRECIOUS ROSARY OF
A WARRIOR OF AWAKENING
ATISHA DIPAMKARA SHRIJNANA

In the practice of Sengueï Ngaro, various transcendent virtues are cultivated. The first of them is the virtue of giving, or generosity. It is recommended to practice the four forms of giving six times every day: gifts of goods, of instruction, of protection, and of love. Among these different forms of giving, it is protection that is most developed in Sengueï Ngaro. According to His Holiness Kalu Rinpoche, this form of giving applies essentially to those who cannot protect themselves and need the help of others.

This is also called the gift of "no fear." It's about a specific form of giving, considered to be a very high form, that is part of the third form of giving and very much higher than the gift of material goods or the gift of dharma. Its aim is to protect beings from fear, from danger, or from death.

This gift of protection can be explained in two ways.

First of all, protecting life is the same as acting with compassion. The act of generosity is not directed toward an object; it's a spontaneous attitude. When you sense the anger or hatred of one individual toward another or toward yourself, or when you see a malevolent behavior being manifested toward someone, it is vital to control this anger or to try to reduce its intensity. This is the practical application and meaning of Sengueï Ngaro. In fact, the real gift rules over the formation and the act that creates it. The act is then not compromised by being necessarily directed toward an object, but instead is like a meditation. The act of generosity, or of the protection of life, must be a spontaneous act that is limitless, unhindered, and uncontrived.

The second way to understand that acting for the protection of life is a form of action motivated by compassion is to observe the activity of accomplished beings. For example, His Holiness Kalu Rinpoche bought many animals during his life, such as birds and turtles that were relegated to spending their lives in captivity or were to be killed, and released them back into nature. This is the spontaneous manifestation of the perfection of the gift of protection, which the great Tibetan masters have always developed naturally.

What's required is to be able to react with either gentleness or firmness as you develop compassion in the course of being protective. Of course, to do this requires a certain amount of courage and skillful means. Such courage is that of the bodhisattva who has taken a vow to struggle against adversity and against all evils that affect the spirit of all beings.

A Senguëï Ngaro proverb states, "You don't put out fire with fire."

In fact, to put out fire you need water, and not fire; if you get angry in order to struggle against anger, you will then only reinforce the adversarial situation, and it would be like pouring oil on the flames. What's needed is to put out the flames of anger with an overflowing of bodhicitta.

The practice of the gift of not fearing amounts to protecting beings from physical violence, just as you would help an animal that has fallen into water, down a cliff, or into a fire, or one caught in a trap.

But not everyone is able to help: for example, a person who is attacked in the subway by five armed individuals.

That's where the benefits of the practice of Senguëï Ngaro come in. Certain beings who don't have the capability of physically helping a person in danger without risking their own lives or the lives of others can, according to Buddhist teachings, pray that the aggressive persons may be freed from their mental disturbances. However, advanced practitioners of the martial art of Senguëï Ngaro may actually, after a few years of practice, be able to intervene physically in certain cases and help those in danger. By acting in this way with fearlessness* and wisdom, they receive as much benefit as the person they are trying to help.

If they act against fear or against negative forces, no obstacle can harm them. This is stated in certain Buddhist texts such as *The Jewel Ornament of Liberation:*

> *If you protect those who are in danger against fear,*
> *No harmful force can touch you*
> *And you will be preeminently strong.*

The name itself of this martial discipline, which is designed to support those who are afraid or who fall prey to a situation of aggression, is "the roaring of the lion." This preeminent form of the lion must animate you, and your intention must be noble and purified of any stain.

The practice of generosity in giving is the first perfection that the Buddha taught. He himself stated that it was like "a jewel that fulfills desire." In making wishes to such a jewel, you can obtain all you desire and be fulfilled; by practicing the gift of protection, your generosity will fulfill the giver and receiver alike.

The practice of the gift of protection engenders, among other things, courage and fearlessness. If you train in the art of Sengueï Ngaro, your bravery will increase little by little, and will become like that of a lion. Certain beings who are animated by a great compassion and who have perfected the gift of protection can be led to give their own lives so that others may live. Offering one's own life, one's own body, as the Buddha did in one of his previous lives to feed starving young tigers, is a courageous act and a supreme gift. But it also brings the wisdom of an activity that can accomplish anything.

Beginning by giving small things, one arrives at such a level of generosity. Then little by little offering more-precious gifts cuts off avarice at its source. Being able to protect someone who is in danger is the

---

*In Tibetan: *jigme.*

practice of a bodhisattva. This martial art must be placed in its original historical context, when it was used first and foremost to protect the life of a precious lama who could be attacked, or whose life might even be in danger. But it is not a question of throwing oneself body and soul into the heart of the battle without being prepared—because by doing that, there would be no benefit for oneself or for anyone else.

This protection will be given in the most useful way, without harm to oneself, from a motivation of real compassion and with a clear vision of reality. The greatest of motivations is bodhicitta, since immeasurable virtues will arise if the gift is made with a pure and limitless motivation.

In Tibet there is, for example, the iconographic representation of the "protectress with the white parasol." She is called in Tibetan Dukkhar,* and she is said to protect all beings against all scourges and adversities. She is the preeminent symbol of protection. Her body is covered with a thousand eyes—symbols of her great compassion—that neglect no feeling creature in difficulty. Her thousand arms symbolize the thousand skillful ways she labors for the protection of beings. This is a protection that is limitless or infinite, and has a thousand faces.

It is possible to think of often risking your life through unlimited giving, and therefore needing to pay attention to this way of giving protection. In fact, the gift of protection is like the gift of material goods. It must be given at the right moment and in the right way; otherwise, huge obstacles will be created, which could endanger your life and the lives of others. Effective protection is like wealth. Wealth has no meaning unless it is given and used to help others who are in difficulty. In addition, just as there is no reason to be attached to your belongings since inevitably you will be separated from them at death without having drawn benefit for having owned them, so also there is no reason for the practitioner of Sengueï Ngaro not to use the art of protection at the moment when he is most in need of it. By acting in this way, the

---

*In Sanskrit this goddess is called Sitatapatra. (See plate 13.)

gift of protection becomes a virtuous mental intention of giving. When this gift of not fearing is practiced with the motivation of bodhicitta, it truly becomes a perfection of the gift.

It is important to be clear about the way this gift of protection is used. One very well might think that just as the gift of wealth eliminates poverty, the gift of protection might also eliminate all aggression. Actually it doesn't necessarily work that way. Unfortunately, most people wield their wealth or their protection as power. Just as certain people are very rich and do not use their riches in a clever manner, so, too, can one use very wrongly this gift of not fearing once it has been cultivated.

If this power of protection is used in a clumsy way, for example, by using it for personal pride, fame, celebrity, or renown so as to be the best, it will become a source of suffering for others. Then no benefit will come from this practice. The Buddha said:

> *Whoever has power*
> *Has a negative karma.*
> *Whoever possesses wealth*
> *Has greed and miserliness.*

This means that the wealthier you become, the more greedy you are and the more attached you are to what you have amassed. Your riches then become a source of problems and a permanent worry, because you become more and more attached to them and never have enough.

There is a story from the time of the Shakyamuni Buddha in which a man who owned a jewel that granted every desire came to ask him who would be the neediest person to whom he could offer this jewel, so that goodness would flow from it. The Buddha suggested that he offer it to an extremely wealthy king in India who owned a thousand wives, a thousand oxen, a thousand palaces, a thousand caves overflowing with gold and precious stones, and so on. By singling out this king, the Buddha knew that the wealthier someone is, the more miserly such a person is, and that the jewel would be more useful to this king than to the poorest of men who, unlike the king, knew how to be happy with very little.

There are two ways of using this power of protection so that it is as useful as possible: first of all, through the perfection of the "free generosity of the three circles." These three circles designate the object toward which an action is directed, or the indirect object; the actor who is the originator of the action; and the direct object of the action. In the case of the gift of protection, this means the individual who receives the gift of protection, the person who gives it, and the protection offered to those who cannot protect themselves and who need another's help (for example, sick people, threatened animals, people who are attacked).

Your gift of protection must be free of intention by being beyond a subject, an object, and an act. Instead it must be a spontaneous generosity that can be compared to love and compassion, since these virtues can be developed without reference to beings or to external reality.

Second, the practice of Sengueï Ngaro must be carried out only through the perfection of generosity for the welfare of others. The power of protection must be actually used for the welfare of others; otherwise, the opportunity for developing compassion is lost. It is very important not to use the martial art of Sengueï Ngaro in a clumsy way by seeking power over others, or by wanting simply to show it off.

This is why no exhibitions are given of this art. My master himself, Lama Tra, always refused to show any single form in its entire sequence. He carried out only one movement after another and showed only what had to be studied and transmitted. Anything that falls into the category of being useless, showy, or spectacular must be eliminated.

Sengueï Ngaro is like a flask of precious perfume of the most subtle fragrance. If opened a little so that it can be noticed in the atmosphere rather than used, it evaporates. And then when you really want to make use of it, only the liquid will remain; the scent will have disappeared, evaporated. The perfume will no longer exist, since its essence will be gone.

How can you lose this essence by giving, even though riches have no meaning unless they are given or used to come to someone's aid?

In fact, there is a natural contradiction in people between being what they desire and knowing how they should behave.

Just as you give your goods at the right moment, which is a moment that does not put any obstacle in the way of your spiritual development and at the same time confers great benefit to those to whom you are giving, in the same way, if you give protection to someone, whatever has been kept in reserve, hidden from others, can then be used at the right moment. It is up to you to judge whether or not you have to give your goods, and whether or not you must use your art of Sengueï Ngaro—even if someone demands that you do.

What counts is motivation. It is much easier to give a few scraps of bread to the pigeons or martial arts instruction in a gym than it is to give a ruby necklace to a beggar or to help a person being attacked with a knife in the street. That's why in Sengueï Ngaro the noblest of motivations is bodhicitta, and the most appropriate way of being helpful to others is boundless compassion.

You can act in all kinds of ways, but what is the right way? The gift of protection in the art of Sengueï Ngaro also requires the development of discipline, which is the second perfection. With discipline, you can really develop the right way of acting along with the development of great and boundless compassion.

☯ Ethical Discipline

> *Keep control over yourself,*
> *Always act with a smile,*
> *Avoid all expression of anger,*
> *Be a friend to others and treat them with uprightness.*
> THE LANDS OF BODHISATTVAS

Why is it necessary to cultivate the perfection of ethical discipline in Sengueï Ngaro? The perfection of ethical discipline is the second of the transcendent perfections. If, for the welfare of others, one wishes to cultivate generosity, and in particular the gift of protection, it is absolutely necessary to apply a discipline so that one is able to refrain from non-virtue and, through this, avoid harming others by what is done physically, verbally, or mentally. Whoever ventures into the jungle of martial arts will surely be lost if he doesn't practice ethical discipline. Ethical discipline is like a compass that indicates the right path, the path of bodhicitta.

Just as with the perfection of not fearing, the perfection of discipline is for the welfare of others. Discipline can be compared to a very fertile field in which all qualities can grow, just like barley. By adopting and then maintaining discipline, the practitioner lays a foundation for all virtues.

So that discipline is most useful and strives toward real perfection, the practitioner must develop a real discipline that prevents him from harming others. This discipline can be called an ethical discipline, because it gathers together all that is virtuous and positive as well as everything that allows living beings to be helped. The Buddhist tradition distinguishes ten virtuous actions that need to be developed, and three types of ethical discipline are mentioned.

First, there is the ethical discipline called "restraint," which consists of avoiding evil.* Then there is the ethical discipline that consists of bringing together everything that is positive. And after that we have the ethical discipline that we develop especially in the practice of Sengueï Ngaro: coming to the aid of sentient beings.

This aspect of ethical discipline is stated in the tradition of Sengueï Ngaro using ten or so rules:

First of all, helping others in a useful way and avoiding incorrect

---

*Essentially this means giving up harming others and letting go of the elements that propel us into doing harm.

behavior (taking the lives of beings, taking what has not been given, and so on); misdeeds of speaking (such as using words that hurt or wound, lying); and having bad thoughts (maintaining erroneous views, being wicked, and things like that). By avoiding these negative acts in one's behavior, it's possible to avoid being the cause of conflict. If, for example, you reply to hurtful words using hurtful words, it will not resolve a conflict. On the contrary, there is the risk of making it much worse.

Similarly, if someone has malicious thoughts about you and you develop the same attitude toward that person, then there is almost no chance to bring about peace, or to reduce or end the conflict.

One day, Lama Tra asked me to keep the following wise counsel in mind and to apply it as often as possible in my daily life: "Avoid brutality and haste, and cultivate a smile as you move through your day."

An important rule consists in relieving the pain of those who suffer. This means bringing a remedy for the suffering, just as a doctor brings medicine to someone who is ill. The medicine must be the right one and must be given in the right dosage. Very often the pill doesn't go down easily, but even if it isn't always nice to swallow, it has the intention of curing suffering. If the intervention is incorrect or too late, the patient can even die.

Very often, a harsh word does nothing to solve a conflict. On the contrary, speaking kindly in a calm and pleasant way, without attachment or hatred, will avoid inappropriate behavior and can perhaps bring calm to situations where there is suffering.

Protecting those who are in danger is also part of the perfection of ethical discipline. This activity must be developed with the motivation of a bodhisattva, and is essential to the application of martial arts techniques.

One day when I was training with my teacher Lama Tra, he saw that I was favoring the martial arts aspect in my execution of the form while neglecting the motivational aspect, so he interrupted me and said calmly, "Our attitude must always be animated by benevolence, since it is because of our enemy that we are able to awaken."

It is important to understand that if people act with anger and their action gives rise to aggressiveness and a situation charged with danger, it is because they are ruled by disturbed emotions and duality.

In such a case, there must be compassion for such beings. You must invoke in yourself the spirit of Awakening and the desire to come to their aid, and to free them from their disturbing emotions. The martial art of the lama warriors was never intended for demonstrations or performances, such as the traditional lama dances of Losar.* This art must be used only when necessary to protect those who are in danger, and to help them while maintaining a benevolent and compassionate attitude.

A teaching of the Venerable Lama Guendun Rinpoche helps call to mind the attitude that is essential and vital to the activity of a bodhisattva. "The essential teaching on the law of cause and effect is as follows: Avoid harboring the slightest trace of malevolence toward others, and remain always in a state of mind that is nothing but helpful. This attitude of mind is absolutely essential."[2]

This is why one of the rules of this form of ethical discipline, a discipline that consists of coming to the aid of others, is to eradicate what is negative. In fact, freeing a person who is under the sway of disturbances—such as anger, for example—does not mean getting angry oneself. Nor does it mean stirring up even more anger in oneself than the other person has, thinking that will resolve the conflict. It's the same with hurtful words: don't set about using more of them than the other person, thinking that by doing so you can come out ahead.

One must be very vigilant so as not to be drawn into anger. This is what it means to act with the perfection of the gift of not fearing, linked with the perfection of the ethical discipline of coming to the aid of sentient beings. Don't let yourself be upset by other people's disturbances. The arousal of the spirit of Awakening will allow you to resolve

---

*Tibetan word meaning "New Year" and the name of the festival celebrating it.

the conflicts around you with wisdom, while giving meaning to what you do without violating the rules of ethical discipline.

I invite you to contemplate the meaning of this prayer, composed by the Venerable Lama Tsongkhapa, which says:

> *Like a mother who cherishes her children,*
> *May I cherish all those who constantly think*
> *Of harming my body, my possessions, and my life,*
> *As well as all those who speak to me in an unpleasant*
> *   way.*
> *Through my practices,*
> *By considering others as my equals,*
> *By putting myself in their place,*
> *As well as by the development of the special attitude,*
> *And the creation of the spirit of Awakening,*
> *May I lead them quickly to enlightenment.*[3]

There are two points to be clarified about the specific rule of truly shutting down what is negative.

The first is that a practitioner of Sengueï Ngaro must always act in a skillful way if he wants to overcome disturbances and thereby achieve the perfection of ethical discipline. It's not about sitting back and doing nothing, because, as the saying goes, "To not oppose evil is to encourage evil."

Second, if the root of the thorny bush is not cut, it will come up again. It is necessary, therefore, to cut off anger at its root, and to really turn your attention to discipline when you engage in Sengueï Ngaro and travel the path toward Awakening. Someone who behaves ethically in thought, word, and deed can be considered an authentic practitioner of Sengueï Ngaro if he knows how to maintain the purity of his discipline.

By engaging in the first form of the discipline, which is avoiding evil, the practitioner accumulates positive deeds such as practicing giving, keeping the precepts in mind, and examining his own mistakes. He then develops the third form of the discipline—gathering together everything positive. This means being at the service of those who are ill, tolerating scorn, guarding the doors of the senses, and so on.

However, it may happen that for one reason or another someone attacks with determination and anger. In order to be able to get through it and put an end to the negativity, very often one will need to come up with an adaptive defensive response that may be as strong as the attack. Also, in wanting to stop the negativity, there is a risk of falling into nonvirtue and stirring up trouble.

In fact, even if the response is proportional to the attack, no martial arts action can be considered nonvirtuous, because the spirit of Awakening makes all action pure. These are three very important points to understand.

First of all, when speaking of this Tibetan martial art of Sengueï Ngaro, which is practiced by Tibetan monks called lama warriors, care must be taken not to misunderstand these words. If one is preoccupied with his own well-being and personal safety, nonvirtue will enter and ethical discipline and the spirit of Awakening will degenerate.

But if there is watchfulness in those actions, it will guard against betraying the bodhisattva vow, which is to help all beings and to mobilize all possible skill to realize this intention. By doing so, neither moral decline nor negative karma occurs in the process of helping other beings while using this martial art.

The second point is that in this martial arts discipline of Sengueï Ngaro, the science of the various vital points of the body is taught to the student right from the beginning. This is done not so that the student will become an expert in manipulating these points, but precisely so that these points can be avoided, or so that their effects are controlled and no one is harmed.

In certain martial arts schools in China and Japan, this kind of teaching is given only after several years of practice, since such knowledge must not fall into every practitioner's hands. In Sengueï Ngaro it's the opposite. Although this science of vital points exists and is taught, it is only so that from the beginning it can be used to avoid the danger of unintentionally touching one of the vital points that are capable of causing paralysis or death.

The third point is that even if you must at all costs save the life of another, or your own life in a situation of extreme danger, you always must remember that mistreating another sentient being is something extremely negative.

It is unacceptable to deviate from ethical discipline by claiming that if the aggressor is gravely wounded or dead, then that's just the way it is: that everything possible was done to avoid it and that any response was motivated entirely by a bodhisattva intention. This is the trap of fanaticism or terrorism. It amounts to a descent into the trap of believing that one's battle against evil is a veritable holy war, and that one's response to evil is both justified and sacred. There are examples in the Crusades, in a jihad, and so on. Tibet, too, has known this type of conflict between schools. It has not been unusual to see the adherents of a school quarreling with each other and going to war over doctrine, in the name of the supremacy of wisdom! Where is the real bodhicitta to be found? Where are we going to find the ethical discipline of coming to the aid of others in an authentic way?

On this point it is critical to be clear that, according to the Buddhist tradition, even if a bodhisattva has to kill, it is not a nonvirtuous action since on an absolute level it has not been carried out for his own survival, but for the welfare of all sentient beings. It is said in the teachings on karma that if a bodhisattva takes a life, he does not accumulate any negative karma because his pure bodhicitta makes his deeds completely pure. This is why bodhicitta is compared to mercury: it whitens all deeds, just as mercury whitens metal.

There is a story based on the previous lives of the Buddha that relates how, while still only a bodhisattva, he was led, with pure bodhicitta motivation, to kill someone, and why he did this.

According to this story, during a previous lifetime the bodhisattva was captain of a large ship that was taking five hundred merchants on a long journey. Using his clairvoyant powers, the bodhisattva saw that one of the merchants was preparing to kill all the others, and he saw, too, that because of this negative act, the merchant would be reborn in hell. The bodhisattva developed a great compassion for the merchant and his future victims, and he decided to kill this merchant and take upon himself the karma of taking a life, rather than abandon the five hundred merchants to their sad fate.

The story makes clear that by acting in this way, the bodhisattva was engaging in two virtuous acts: he was avoiding a rebirth in hell for the wicked merchant and he was protecting the life of all the other occupants of his ship. Through this action, the bodhisattva was fostering simultaneously the perfection of protection and the perfection of ethical discipline; he was coming to the aid of others and achieving, through what he was doing for them, a considerable advancement toward Awakening. It is important not to misunderstand the meaning of this story—the act of killing is contrary to the right way of acting when coming to help others in a real way.

One might also contemplate the injunctions of His Holiness the Dalai Lama, who has always encouraged Tibetan resistance fighters not to choose the way of violence and never to kill, even though their actions are motivated by the liberation of their country. Lama Bui also chose the way of nonviolence and left his monastery without spilling blood or even expressing the least anger toward the Chinese soldiers who were murdering his fellow monks.

☯ Patience

> *The stick is what is really hitting me.*
> *Instead of getting angry with the person wielding it,*
> *And who also is an instrument, because he is moved by*
> *   hatred,*
> *It is really the hatred that I must oppose.*
>
> BODHISATTVACHARYAVATARA
>
> SHANTIDEVA

Developing patience allows you to not get angry. Numerous obstacles, both inner and outer, can crop up in life. You need to be extremely patient in relation to these hostilities, and make efforts to develop this important virtue called patience. Patience is anger's antidote.

Getting angry with someone not only destroys all positive energy and merit, but is also the main reason that the exercise of patience gets damaged. In the sutras we find it said that a single moment of anger can destroy all accumulated merit.

This is why you must strive to maintain a peaceful state of mind— happy and caring toward others even if they have malicious thoughts toward you, or if they get angry and want to put you down, or even if their hostility puts you in physical danger.

It is certainly difficult to stoically accept the slander and suffering that others inflict without reacting or responding!

However, to prevent a feeling of discontent from lodging wthin, the best remedy is to stoically endure the suffering inflicted by others and con- sider the benefits of patience. Many great masters in the past, notably in the Kagyu lineage, subjected their pupils to dreadful trials, such as the trials the yogi Tilopa subjected his student Naropa to in order to test his patience. How many people complain every day that they can't stand the slightest dis- tress or deprivation, or even the smallest of arguments. Patience is the war- rior's weapon that allows misfortune to be transformed into a spiritual path regardless of whether the misfortune is inflicted directly or indirectly—by beings who stray into duality or illusion (bound by ignorance and ego) or by obstacles or interruptions that impede progress in the practice of Sengueï Ngaro. Patience is the ability to withstand, through trust, compassion, and an understanding of emptiness, all suffering and adversity.

And not yielding to frustration means applying the following advice of Geshe Langri Thangpa, recorded in the *Eight Verses on Training the Mind:*

> *I will take defeat upon myself,*
> *And give victory to others.*

This relates to the Taoist martial arts expression:

If you want to be the victor, don't fight!

This thought of Lao Tzu's is very close to the concept of patience in Sengueï Ngaro. Actually, getting angry and fighting serves no purpose. Getting so annoyed and being so unhappy that you begin to fight does nothing but make the mind bitter, and doesn't change an aggressive situation into a peaceful one. Most often it only makes things worse! Being patient means remaining unwavering and unshakable in the state called *miyowa* in Sengueï Ngaro. This doesn't imply being weak; on the contrary, patience is an enormous force, as His Holiness the Dalai Lama often reiterates.

Therefore, adversity must be considered an advantage on the spiritual path. Every time that suffering and negativity arise, you owe it to yourself to develop a sincere attitude that will act as a help in creating virtue. You need to think this way: "From the moment an unfavorable and harmful circumstance arises, I will use skillful means that allow me to extract real benefit from it." Patience must be your only guide.

For example, if you're suffering from an illness and you begin to groan and take the suffering seriously and turn in upon yourself, you will end up doing nothing but complaining, and the suffering will increase more and more. Instead of being the victor, you will be vanquished. It is said in the Tibetan medical tantras that sometimes recovery from an illness depends a great deal on the patience of the person who is ill. Not allowing yourself to be affected by suffering is a specific training in Sengueï Ngaro, since it allows you to develop patience. Through patience you will develop other virtues as well, such as not fearing and courage, as well as conditioning and endurance.

By becoming more and more patient, you enjoy a tranquil and peaceful life, even when living in the heart of an aggressive, oppressive, and stressful locale.

What is the relationship between patience and courage?

When faced with a frightening aggressor, you can redouble your courage even if you are not as strong as your aggressor, or are wounded from the conflict. This is true because the continual practice of patience, which has been developed through a program of training and meditation, will have conferred on you a resoluteness of spirit and an unshakable determination. Even the least enemy or the slightest wound will be unable to be an obstacle or destroy the potential for positive energy.

You will continue to be able to accomplish positive acts even in very hostile situations, since it will not be possible for even the deepest awkwardness to cause you significant suffering. This amounts to the development of bodhisattva courage.

Courage is the capacity to withstand obstacles and trials without creating disturbances. The one who is "courageous" then becomes a "hero," since he has managed to overcome the real obstacle: anger. In fact, the root cause essentially comes back to anger.

If it happens that someone approaches and hits you forcefully with a stick, why get angry with the stick that hit you instead of, more logically, going after the one who was wielding it? But that person is controlled by anger. Logically, then, you need to go after the anger! By pondering in this way, you will be able to attain perfect control of your emotions and no longer counter violence with violence. In Tibet there are many stories that relate the ways in which great masters were able to help their disciples control anger and develop absolute bodhicitta. Some of them even succeeded in attaining Awakening at the same time that they conquered anger.

In the Buddhist way of thinking, instead of being upset with a person who harbors ill will or is aggressive, it is better to display deep affection, or even sincere respect. Such a person is highly valued and considered to be like a best friend. The great yogi Milarepa praised all forms of obstacles that came his way, since they helped him develop bodhicitta and patience. "May all obstacles and enemies be praised, since they are truly gifts."

So then you must accept adversity without experiencing either agitation or disappointment, and look upon your enemies with affection and gratitude. Enemies offer the most valuable gift: the rare opportunity to really practice patience. This is real practice. And it's also the profound message of compassion that His Holiness the Dalai Lama teaches throughout the world.

If you combat anger and hatred by practicing patience, you will succeed in containing the process at its source. Just as the flow of a powerful river can be cut off by diverting it at its source, so, too, can anger be prevented from arising by eliminating feelings of discontent, lack of self-control, or dissatisfaction.

His Holiness the Dalai Lama makes clear that anger and hatred are fed by discontent, by upsetting feelings of dissatisfaction, and by the impression that something is not quite right. Looking more deeply, this discontent and feeling of dissatisfaction actually arise from duality and from relating to the world through the experience of attachment, aversion, or indifference. But taking a stand within duality arises from the clinging to self, from ego. By being more open to others and constantly cultivating a spirit of relative and ultimate Awakening, it's possible to replace this clinging to self—this ego—with love and compassion, and to be able to see the inherent emptiness of the nature of self and of all phenomena.

☯ Effort

> *The lives of beings of these evil times are short.*
> *They are slow to rouse themselves to make efforts, and*
> *their perseverance is feeble,*
> *While, at the same time, their laziness and distractions*
> *are far-reaching.*
> *Alas! How heartbreaking!*
>
> PREDICTION OF GURU RINPOCHE[4]

The perfection of effort is characterized by the enthusiasm and joy a practitioner of Sengueï Ngaro generates when he endeavors to do good in his sphere. He must always develop this perseverance in a natural way during his training in the various martial arts techniques.

The practitioner really begins to generate this lively perseverance when the training is no longer a constraint or a burden, when there isn't anything that appears useless or unnecessary. For this lively perseverance to lead to a full realization of the goal, it's important to do more than occasional practice or halfhearted efforts; one must develop a keen effort.

In fact, the perfection of effort is at the heart of all other practices. All the perfections are characterized by this notion of developing what is the highest, most elevated good. Of course, this path requires a real effort and does not suit everyone. Backed by the spirit of Awakening, this effort can support the accumulation of merit and the bestowing of virtue of all kinds. The degree of effort follows from the extent of motivation. When pure, this motivation alone can help others and allow the practitioner to achieve a state of illumination.

In the individual spirit, virtue is the cause of happiness, but virtue is weak compared to the disturbing emotions that are the cause of so much unconscious suffering. That's just the way we are. The disturbing emotions are very strong and powerful, which means that they can bring about certain effects without any effort.

From another point of view, this elusive happiness that everyone is looking for is very hard to find. In vain do we work, with efforts leading nowhere, whereas suffering seems to arise all by itself.

It is just because suffering arises on its own and happiness is difficult to attain that one must cultivate the perfection of effort. Only through that can happiness be achieved. The Buddha advises not to look for it outside oneself, but to nurture it within. A Tibetan proverb tells us not to look for the elephant in the forest when it is quietly curled up within.

Of course, fostering such an effort is difficult. There are two essential points about it:

First of all, this effort concerns the practitioner's spirit, which delights in virtuous deeds, notably the ability to come to the aid of others through the gift of protection. This kind of effort, when it arises from the motivation of the spirit of Awakening, is then a perfection of effort.

Making this kind of effort is not something extra to be added on to regular practice, nor is it a perfection to be practiced separately. Actually, just as the shadow accompanies the body in all its movements, this effort accompanies all virtuous deeds. However, if a lot of energy is wasted on nonvirtuous or neutral acts, true happiness remains elusive; such behavior cannot be considered to be a practice of effort.

Second, fostering this kind of effort is assuredly very difficult. In fact, it's at the heart of what effort is: if there weren't difficulties, there would be no need to make efforts. If there were no suffering to overcome, there would be no merit in training oneself in a path of renunciation and virtue.

When the Buddha himself was faced with temptation by Mara, who is a personification of death, Mara addressed the bodhisattva in this way:

> *The pathway of effort is difficult, difficult to follow and*
> *difficult to attain.**

Thus if it takes only the difficulty of effort to hold one back, one can certainly falter, probably give up midway, or even move in the opposite direction. However, if one makes an effort and it is accompanied by virtuous conduct, one will certainly overcome laziness. In this way, one no longer will be able to go off in the opposite direction out of discouragement, or find oneself falling into futility or adversity that is without virtue.

---

*Lalita Vistara. This story is not about Mara's assaults on the day of the Buddha's enlightenment, but about one of Mara's temptations that took place during the six years of austerity at Uruvela.

Without slackening his effort, the Buddha responded to Mara in these terms:

> *Dying in battle*
> *Is better than living vanquished.*
> *The hero put the army to rout.*

In this discourse, the Buddha describes the various armies that assail the world, teaching that it is necessary to overcome through wisdom, just as running water dissolves a bowl made of fresh clay. The first army is lechery. Then comes loathing. The third is hunger and thirst. The fourth is desire. The fifth is laziness and indolence; the sixth, fear. The seventh is none other than doubt, which is followed by anger and hypocrisy. Then there are property and fame, honor and false glory, and praise for oneself and scorn for others.

In order to overcome these armies, one needs to do battle. And battle cannot be waged without effort and without the perfection of this effort. This is why in traditional texts the Buddha is called the "hero who is victorious in battle."

There is a double reason for practicing this perfection of effort. On the one hand, there is the opportunity and possibility now of studying and practicing the art of Sengueï Ngaro, and of meeting masters in this martial arts path. This can help bring clarity about what is beneficial and what is not, and shows the benefits of the teaching of Sengueï Ngaro. This is why it seems wise and necessary for a practitioner of this art to remain watchful and continue to maintain effort in order to guard against laziness, bad habits, or some ill-advised practice.

On the other hand, there is another reason to practice the virtue of correct and right effort. Right effort is one of the eight spokes of the wheel of the teaching of Buddha. This wheel is called *dharmachakra,* "the wheel of law." When the Buddha gave his first discourse, he spelled out four truths. In describing the fourth among them, which he named "the noble truth on the path that leads to the cessation of suffering," he spelled out that it consisted in following the noble eightfold path: right view, right intention, right speech, right action, right livelihood, right effort, right mindfulness (right attention), right concentration. It is said that it was from this moment that the Buddha set in motion the wheel of the teaching.*

The symbolism of the eight spokes of the wheel of dharma can also be found in the eight-pointed star of Yoga Tchouzar, at the heart of the art of Sengueï Ngaro. Described among these teachings are the four stages of mindfulness, the four right efforts, the four powers of the mind, the five spiritual faculties, the five powers, the seven factors of enlightenment, and the noble eightfold path. The Buddha has stated this in order to make clear that effort must be practiced in a skillful way, and that effort must be united with perseverance. In this way, a practitioner can achieve the Buddha state, even if it takes several lifetimes.

However, very often it happens that a practitioner develops a lot of effort and enthusiasm at the beginning of training, then quits when big gains haven't been made. This kind of effort can be compared to a torrent that descends from the mountain for a short time due to a violent storm.

In contrast, when a practitioner develops a continuous effort and gently cultivates perseverance while steadily wishing to progress toward Awakening, regardless of the time and effort required to carry out this wish, his effort can be compared to a mighty river that flows day and night all year long without interruption. This is why the practice of Sengueï Ngaro distinguishes among four kinds of effort based on the intensity of practice.

In fact, being patient is not enough. Enthusiastic perseverance must

---

*The Buddha himself stated that this teaching of the noble eightfold path was an integral part of his teachings and practices. It's not enough to simply be aware of the path. The practices and teachings were taught for the benefit and happiness of all, out of compassion for the world and beneficence. We must learn them, follow them, practice them, and cultivate them. One of the eight spokes of the wheel is right effort.

be perfected in order to accumulate merit. It is said that just as there is no movement without wind, merit is not produced without perseverance or courage. This is why, in speaking of courage, enthusiasm, or even perseverance, one might feel unable or unsuited to enter into this difficult path of the perfection of effort. Actually, any person can succeed by developing certain qualities such as perfect intention, and even energy, steadfastness, and so on. In fact, this courage is also called "joyous effort," and can be divided into four categories:

"Armor-clad effort" refers to the act of doing good without being discouraged. This means not leaving beneficial courage behind, and not slackening one's pace or becoming discouraged. That's why this first effort is also called "perfect intention." This "armor-clad effort" or "armor-clad courage" is a real determination to make it through any trial. Such an effort develops the moment a virtuous act is undertaken, for example, coming to the aid of someone being physically attacked.

"Vigorous effort" involves the development of substantial energy for virtuous practices of the moment. It involves giving up negative emotions and developing the effort of doing good for others while acting with joy and diligence. At this stage, this kind of effort aims to assemble virtuous practices. "Vigorous effort" is cultivated when one truly want to make progress in the practice of Sengueï Ngaro.

"Steady effort" is characterized by the stable mind that arises from long-term, regular practice. Here the practitioner really develops effort. When this kind of effort is fostered, five qualities naturally appear: steadfastness, enthusiasm, imperturbability, irrevocable determination, and humility. These five qualities of effort are essential for the practice of Sengueï Ngaro and its direct application during a situation of conflict.

"Rigorous effort" is the act of always accomplishing more without complacency. This real effort is accompanied by humility.

It is also called "insatiable effort," because at this stage the practitioner never feels satisfied with the good he has been able to accomplish, and he constantly develops more virtuous actions. This type of insatiable effort applies in a basic way to the art of Sengueï Ngaro, since it is above all a question of coming to the aid of sentient beings. This kind of courage is characterized by the aspiration of really helping all those who are in danger or whom no one is helping.

Developing such an effort is the sign that one's perseverance is correct. Such perseverance may be termed "right perseverance," since it basically arises from renunciation and from the wisdom of the nonself. This kind of effort is directed solely toward doing good. Since it quickly brings higher knowledge, it is like the heavenly steed that can transport the practitioner to a mythical land near the great ocean.

☯ Concentration

> *Without acting, the body naturally quiet,*
> *Without saying a word, words like a nonempty echo,*
> *Without thinking, thought moves on into the dharma of*
>   *the beyond.*

TILOPA, MAHAMUDRA INSTRUCTIONS

When someone begins in the art of Sengueï Ngaro, the mind is often disturbed and easily distracted. In order to gradually eliminate mental dispersion, it's necessary to develop attention and watchfulness, which allows for a completely peaceful state. This state of mind is called *shinay* in Tibetan. *Shi* means "peace, repose." *Nay* means that one remains in a state of peace, free from agitation.

Attention and an absence of mental dispersion go hand in hand, and one cannot arise without the other. Specifically, the absence of mental dispersion is said to be the cause of attention.

These two practices bring the capability of really observing the mind and its mode of operation. To obtain this capability, you need to meditate on the suffering inherent in the cycle of lives, and on impermanence as well. Without a deep understanding of the nature of reality, it will be especially difficult to purify yourself of the clinging to self. Practicing concentration will lead to the dropping of nonvirtuous actions. This is why, in order to create tranquillity, you must recognize remedies right from the beginning.

In the tradition of Sengueï Ngaro, the practice of concentration takes place in several stages. What is recommended at the beginning is to adopt a correct seated posture—one defined by seven points—then basically to practice this concentration in movement. There are specific exercises for this. (See "Postures of Standing Meditation," in chapter 5.) After a few months, or even a few years, of training, the mind gradually becomes clearer and the state of concentration increases correspondingly.

This allows you to remain in a state of complete peace, and to not fall into agitation when faced with an aggressive and tense situation. The ultimate goal is to achieve a union of mental calm, shiné, with the profound insight called, in Tibetan, *lhaktong*. It is absolutely necessary to develop concentration, both at rest and in movement. You must not allow yourself to be overcome by reluctance, fear, or preoccupation, because these impediments will block a spontaneous response in any situation.

Perfect concentration is indicated in several ways, but mainly by the ability to be completely at one with the present situation. This capability combines various qualities, such as attention, fearlessness, and even opening with the spirit of Awakening.

Depending on the situation that arises, one's response to it will contain various qualities. If bodhicitta, the spirit of Awakening, is developed, certain of these qualities will appear spontaneously.

- Attention is the quality of observation stripped of all hindrance and any conceptual overlay. It comes from the practice of meditation. It is not an attention that is rigid and cut off from the world;

it is a clarity in each situation that fosters direct and authentic perception of reality.

- Fearlessness is a lionlike attitude that is like confidence. Usually when facing an aggressor, the response is to go to pieces or to look for domination or superiority by blocking the situation. Directing it right away toward a concern helps to overcome fear or lack of assurance.

- Acting with fearlessness requires a lion's confidence. The lion doesn't need to manifest his strength outwardly or appear other than he is in order to take control. He only has to roar and this roaring is the sign of fearlessness. The roaring forces a direct, simple, and spontaneous response—perfect action. This is the true perfection of concentration.

- Opening is a way of being, not a state of letting go, or of lethargy. This state of lucid presence brings a precise knowledge based on confidence and self-mastery. If you fear you will drown in the situation, developing fearlessness will not be enough unless you also develop opening. Being open is to be free of fixation, to be transparent, like space.

The second sign of the attainment of perfect concentration will be heralded by the abandonment of attachment to friends and aversion to enemies. Only at such a moment will you know that your mind is at peace. There are specific meditations that allow attainment of this meditative balance, especially in a situation of conflict or when faced with a confrontive aggressor. These meditations keep the mind focused on the ultimate nature of reality, and overcome disturbances and aggression. Enlivened by a fearless, attitude, the mind remains free and without worry.

Traditionally, five obstacles that can arise during martial arts practice are described. Eight remedies are used to eliminate these obstacles. The five obstacles are laziness, forgetting instructions, dullness and agitation, nonintervention, and intervention.

- Laziness: this prevents an engagement with activity by always postponing practice. It may also show up as lack of interest in applying oneself to the training. Some people practice one day and then not another; others practice for a time and then let it drop.
- Forgetting instructions: this involves losing sight of one's goal— for example, having a particular martial arts form to carry out but then not remembering the teacher's instructions on the meaning of the form being practiced.
- Dullness and agitation: during concentration the practitioner encounters two major obstacles, which may be subtle or coarse. First of all is dullness, which opposes clarity and intensity; second is agitation, which opposes stability and calm. These oppositions can confuse the practitioner, who may believe he's in a state of total, right concentration when he isn't at all.
- Nonintervention: we speak of nonintervention when a remedy is not applied and one gives up. Not using appropriate countermeasures is the basis of laziness.
- Intervention: when concentration has been established in the mind and neither dullness nor agitation disturbs it but in spite of that the practitioner continues to make use of remedies and methods for overcoming obstacles, such intervention and application of remedies harm the concentration. In fact, such remedies are no longer useful. Perfecting the application of the martial art of Sengueï Ngaro depends above all on overcoming this obstacle.

By eliminating these five forms of impediments, attainment of the perfection of concentration will be accomplished. Various meditation practices in the art of Sengueï Ngaro prepare the mind to approach emptiness. If the practitioner comes closer to an understanding of this, it can be said that he is on the path of the perfection of wisdom,* which is the ultimate goal of the development of concentration. This is the sixth perfection.

---

*The *Prajnaparamita*.

☯ Transcendent Wisdom

> *When we come to know emptiness,*
> *We strive to do good.*
>
> THE JEWEL ORNAMENT

The perfection of great wisdom is very important in the practice of Sengueï Ngaro, because wisdom is the sole means of lessening one's own suffering and that of others. By joining wisdom with mental calm, it is possible to attain ultimate truth. Generating wisdom develops a virtuous mind and banishes doubt and confusion.

But it is only by practicing wisdom with the pure motivation of bodhicitta that there is the perfection of wisdom.

In the art of Sengueï Ngaro, one of the methods for increasing wisdom is Yoga Tchouzar. Yoga Tchouzar develops a meditative balance based on emptiness, and enables the comprehension of ultimate truth devoid of dualistic appearance. In this way, it becomes possible to distinguish very clearly what is virtuous from what is not, and to know what to practice and what not to practice. Wisdom brings light on the path of spiritual practice.

This is why numerous Buddhist texts set forth the qualities of transcendent wisdom and the consequences of its lack. In this connection, it is said, "Like the inestimable elephant that destroys the enemy, this wisdom has the power to rein in ideas about the real existence of the self and of phenomena."

Without this wisdom the practitioner of Sengueï Ngaro would be without a guide. He would be like a blind man who can't find his way and is unable to reach the town to which he's traveling. Even though he has generosity, patience, and concentration, if the practitioner lacks wisdom, he cannot attain the ultimate goal of omniscience. In contrast, when transcendent wisdom is present along with all the other virtues, it is like a guide leading a multitude of the blind along the path of Awakening.

This image means that without wisdom as a guide, the five other perfections will be blind and cannot be useful, because they cannot lead as far as the final destination: enlightenment.

It is important to be clear that there is a difference between wisdom and the martial arts techniques. In the sequence of Sengueï Ngaro teachings, the *excellent techniques* (Yoga Tchouzar) come after the *secret martial arts techniques based on animals* (Dun Dro Tchou). This means that even if one has all the skills and yet is short on wisdom, the skills will bring next to nothing. On the other hand, in knowing how to maintain a tranquil mind and follow a virtuous path, one is able to dispense with all martial arts techniques and hold above all to a vision that will allow attainment of the direct realization of ultimate reality.

It is necessary to distinguish intelligence from wisdom. Unless wisdom is included in the martial art of Sengueï Ngaro, any understanding of its goal would be incomplete. In this sense, Sengueï Ngaro is distinct from similar disciplines, since it is not concerned solely with acquiring martial arts techniques.

In certain disciplines, there may be great intelligence in the martial arts sphere but very little wisdom in its application. In the Japanese art of Ninjitsu for example, a great many weapons of destruction have been invented, and some of them are very ingenious from a martial arts or worldly point of view, but they contribute no virtue or wisdom to that art. They exist only to bring destruction and death.

In the art of Sengueï Ngaro, wisdom must be practiced in ways that are inseparable from the martial art itself. When wisdom is practiced with the motivation of the spirit of Awakening, there is perfection of wisdom. Otherwise wisdom does not lead to the tranquillity of mind that can distinguish what it is wise to practice and what is not. This leads only to war and the art of waging it, and not to peace and the art of maintaining it. It would be quite wrong to believe that the term "lama warrior" refers to the kind of monk who devotes himself to the art of war. The primary struggle in which he is engaged is with his own mind and with anger. Above all, he must come to emptiness.

It is important to induce this tranquillity of mind in a natural way, even if that may seem difficult. But what is difficult above all is to have emptiness be born of itself, from its own force. This is why one needs to seek instruction from a teacher who has come to this emptiness in a perfectly correct way. Such methods of meditating on emptiness are included in the excellent practices of Senguei Ngaro, and are described in the texts of the *Prajnaparamita* in a profound and detailed manner.

In order to explain to me the difficulty of having emptiness be born of itself, my teacher often gave me the example of a little bird who has just been hatched. The bird cannot fly right away; it takes a long time for that. What provides protection to the baby bird is the care and generosity of its parents, who give it strength by bringing food. The act of continually remaining in the nest symbolizes diligence; patience is the act of providing continual warmth and love to this baby bird. It is not ignored. Then, when its body is stronger and more robust and the baby bird has matured through the five perfections, it is able to fly. This is what constitutes wisdom. When we have achieved the five perfections, we can in the same way move toward the state of Buddha. This means that when we have achieved wisdom, the five other virtues will be achieved at the same time.

The text of the *The Heart of the Prajnaparamita* says:

> *Go, go, go beyond,*
> *Go totally beyond . . .*

Getting to the goal means going way beyond emotion, with no need of recourse to remedies or martial arts techniques. One really comes to the accumulation of wisdom at the moment one comes to the nature of emptiness. This is the path called "accumulation." The practitioner travels this road with the ten lands,* and when he has abandoned that which is most ultimate,† he then attains Buddha nature.‡

---

*In Sanskrit: *bhoumi.*
†In Tibetan: *sang,* everything abandoned.
‡In Tibetan: *gye,* the blossoming of all qualities, the three or the five bodies of a Buddha.

1. Posture for sitting meditation.

2. Posture of the immutable.

3. Posture of the snow lion

4. *The Buddha Sengueï Ngaro.*
Thangka representation of the
Buddha "the Roaring Lion"
consecrated by His Holiness
Karmapa Ogyèn Trinley Dordjé.
His Holiness the Seventeenth
Gyalwang Karmapa, who long
considered himself the reincarnation
of Buddha "Sengueï Ngaro" is
equally named the "Sixth Lion"
(Seng Druk). His Holiness has
blessed this thangka and written his
signature in gold letters above the
flaming cintamani (jewel), symbol
of the Awakening, which answers
all good wishes.

5. *Séngtchèn Norbu*
Dradul. Thangka, Tibet,
seventeenth century,
28 × 36 cm.

6. Djampel Yang. Thanka, Tibet, eighteenth century, 15 × 20 cm.

7. Guru Rinpoche.
Gilded bronze,
Tibet, sixteenth
century, 14 cm.

8. Ling Gesar
Herouka.
Thangka, Tibet,
seventeenth
century,
35 × 53 cm.

*9. Dordjé Drolo.
Tsakli, miniature
painting on
cotton, Tibet,
eighteenth century,
8 × 11 cm.*

*10. Vajra Dakkini
Herouka. Thangka,
Tibet, seventeenth
century, 58 × 40 cm.*

11. *Nechung Dordjé Drakden. Tibetan painting, seventeenth century, 21 ×
17 cm.*

12. Deouatchen. Thangka, Tibet, eighteenth century, 43 × 48 cm.

13. Dukkhar
Tchenma. Thangka,
Tibet, seventeenth
century, 54 × 74 cm.

14. Tchana Dordjé.
Thangka, Tibet,
seventeenth century,
76 × 58 cm.

This is the explanation of the word Buddha in Tibetan—Sang-gye—the one who has attained profound and transcendent wisdom: the *prajnaparamita.**

The qualities of this wisdom have been summarized by the Buddha in three volumes of eighty thousand stanzas, then in a single volume, and finally in *The Heart of the Prajnaparamita,* also known as *The Heart Sutra.* This transcendent virtue of knowledge is kept secret, since it essentially reveals spontaneous wisdom. It was originally guarded as a precious treasure by the king of the *nagas,* a bodhisattva who loved the dharma.

In short, the *Prajnaparamita* states that all appearances are deceptive, like an illusion or a mirage. It is the wisdom of what is beyond objects that can be conceived by the intellect and is free from cessation or noncessation, free of origination, free of dwelling place, free of all forms, sounds, odors, and so on. It is ineffable, unimaginable, and inexpressible. It is not material and not intangible; it is emptiness. Its nature is like the blue of the sky. Such a nature is what is called "the perfection of wisdom."

However, a simple, intellectual knowledge of transcendent wisdom is definitely not enough. One needs to meditate and perfect it by fostering transcendent knowledge.

And yet, since such knowledge seems to be beyond all forms and be inexpressible, how can it be fostered in Sengueï Ngaro? A great yogi of the Kagyu lineage, Gampopa, stressed in his text, *The Jewel Ornament of Liberation,* how difficult it would be to cultivate this knowledge if everything were emptiness.

He put forth the image of silver ore. Until the ore is melted down and refined, the silver remains invisible. This means that even though all things are emptiness since time without end, and are free of all intellectual conceptualization, the beings who people the universe all have different perceptions of reality that cause them to endure various

---

*The perfection of wisdom, the wisdom of all buddhas.

forms of suffering. This is why Gampopa stressed how critical it is to meditate on this knowledge and cultivate it.

The methods are described in four phases:

- The preliminary stages of training the mind to remain in a natural state, free of all conceptualization.
- Meditation, which, as a second stage, leaves the mind as it is without distraction or correction. This is the most difficult phase—not analyzing and having no thought—difficult because the mind is constantly conditioned to come and go. At this stage it is necessary to tame the mind the way one tames an elephant, so that it becomes stable. As the mind dissolves into a space free from elaboration, it is then possible to cultivate transcendent knowledge.
- Next comes the third stage, which consists in cultivating this wisdom "between meditations." In the art of Sengueï Ngaro, it is very important to work intently in between training sessions and meditation practice. These times are for practicing the five kinds of perfection as much as possible, in order to accumulate merit.

  Therefore, even if you're at the sixth perfection, which is beyond the first five, you need to continue to practice the other five so that the accumulation of merit is carried on with no break. If you appropriately apply yourself to practice under the master's direction and yet don't apply the five virtues, when you come to the phases following meditation it will not be good. You will never become accustomed to differentiating meditation from what comes after meditation, and there's a real danger in that.

  I've known, for example, young martial arts practitioners who would press the elevator button with their feet! Others make a soccer ball out of their outfits once their training is over, or they get into a fight as soon as the first aggressive situation comes along. For this reason, Sengueï Ngaro puts a great deal of stress on the five perfections and points out the fact that there is not a single one of the practices that is not included in the attainment of emptiness. Before one seeks to protect one's own life or the life of others, one would do better to cultivate emptiness, even if it's for a single moment, or perhaps even an entire day. As the Buddhist teachings tell us, this is very important. The sutra "Expansion of the Great Realization" spells this out as follows:

> *It is more important to enter into concentration*
> *For one moment than to protect the life*
> *Of all beings of the three worlds.*

The Buddhist teachings say that if the practitioner applies himself to cultivating each perfection along with all the others, he will be able to speed up the process of the attainment of the two accumulations: merit and wisdom. This is the true path of the bodhisattvas that leads to liberation and enlightenment.

With the aim of completely attaining transcendent wisdom most quickly, and accumulating great merit in so doing, the practitioner of Sengueï Ngaro must strive to practice each of the perfections along with all the others. This will provide a multitude of possibilities for accumulating powerful merits.

For example, if a practitioner of Sengueï Ngaro embarks on the practice of this martial art without egotistical or scheming self-interest, without expecting anything in return, he is going to develop the perfection of the gift of protection. Seeking benefit for others above all, he will direct his practice based on bodhicitta and natural goodness, and will combine the perfection of giving with that of ethical discipline. By not cultivating anger toward the obstacles he will encounter on this difficult path, and by accepting the trials and pitfalls he encounters in the course of his double apprenticeship of working with his teacher and traversing the experiences of life, he cultivates the perfection of giving combined with that of patience. Through the joy of giving teachings and through developing energy and endurance during his training, he will combine the perfection of the gift of protection with that of effort. And in developing concentration on right action, which allows him to bring Awakening (from either a relative or absolute point of view) and the absence of suffering to others, he will combine the perfection of giving with that of mental stability. By becoming aware that the giver, the receiver, the action of giving, and what is given (protection) all share the nature of emptiness, he will combine the perfection of giving with that of wisdom. This is also true for the other perfections.

- The fourth and last phase is that of signs of familiarization. When the practitioner cultivates transcendent knowledge, he obtains results—the fruit of his effort. Ultimately this is Awakening, but even on the relative plane he obtains great benefit: absence of hatred, attention to the smallest suffering, a desire to do good for those nearby, less anger, and less reaction to negative emotions.* The practitioner develops unequaled compassion for all beings, builds a sincere renunciation of all distractions of the mind, and devotes himself diligently to the practice of Sengueï Ngaro. Thus, enormous benefits arise from the perfection of transcendent knowledge.†

THE WISDOM OF SENGUEÏ NGARO

☉ *From Anger to Compassion*

How should a practitioner of Sengueï Ngaro react when someone appears, perhaps armed, as an enemy in front of him, and when anger and hatred impel that person to fight?

---

*In Tibetan: *ngö mong pa.*
†In the text of the *Prajnaparamita,* many of these benefits for all beings are spelled out.

Before knowing what is the right action, it is essential to understand why this situation of conflict takes place. His Holiness Kalu Rinpoche has said, "It's not weapons that make war, but the people who use them."

In fact, it's people's minds that produce aggression, anger, and hatred. And this aggression leads to war. Disarming an aggressor will not eliminate conflict, aggressiveness, or anger.

There are remedies against anger, such as meditating on patience or on love toward the enemy, but what is essential is to work at the level of the individual mind, because it is in this mind that the emotions arise.

The cause of aggression can very often be something other than anger. One of the teachings of Sengueï Ngaro elaborates on the various ways in which aggressiveness can arise, how it manifests (through various forms and stages), and how to remedy it by using the appropriate means designed to transform each type of confrontation into a situation of peace.

There are numerous causes behind confrontation—pride, attachment, and jealousy, for example. His Holiness Kalu Rinpoche said, "The fundamental cause of aggression and conflict is emotional instability in the minds of individuals."

It can arise from pride. An individual or a representative of a martial art who thinks he's braver than others will want to prove it by eliminating his competitors, or by challenging them. This is the world of sport and competition. Some individuals go so far as to eliminate their opponents without even respecting the rules of their game or the conventions of their competition.

Emotional instability can also take the form of attachment or desire. Wanting to run off with something that belongs to someone else by deception, force, or extreme violence can be the cause of conflict or aggression. In the case of jealousy, there is fear that the other person will become stronger than oneself, and might cause harm in the future, so he is eliminated right away.

Each of these forms of aggression appears through various types of confrontation at individual, national, or international levels.

In Sengueï Ngaro, one learns to quickly recognize the cause of aggression based on the aggressor's attitude: his body and his words will give away his emotional state of mind before he has even attacked. For example, an aggressor who appears with an emotion of overbearing pride will have his feet less firmly anchored on the ground, his chin will be tilted up, and his movements will be more exaggerated than usual. He lacks rapid movement and protection, since he is not sufficiently aware of the person he is confronting. His complete preoccupation is his self-image and the way he's going to conquer his opponent.

All of this will unfold differently if the aggressiveness is caused by attachment, jealousy, or another emotion.

In fact, all these emotions of conflict can be felt within one's own psyche; it isn't necessary for there to be two people in a situation. If you observe yourself and observe all your daily conflicts at different levels (family, social, professional), you will be able to clearly distinguish the causes of verbal or physical confrontation.

The most terrible aggression does not show up in the body or words, but remains within the psyche. It can be more violent than physical aggression. Certain individuals come to the point of harboring unimaginable hatred toward others, often those close to them, to the point of wanting to eliminate them. Many of these people do not manage to express this violence outwardly. This condition can give rise to huge emotional anguish, which can manifest at different levels ranging from stress to suicide when it remains inside and from murder to genocide when directed outward. This is why numerous writings of the Buddha recommend guarding the doorways of the body, of speech, and of the mind, and not committing any act of evil in word, thought, or deed.

In Sengueï Ngaro, there is also a distinction between cold anger and hot anger, and advice as to how the individual can avoid shifting from one to the other.

The energy shift during aggression can be enormous, and the way the conflict can be resolved will depend on the exact moment when extreme anger is transformed into extreme compassion. Here the image is of the cloud of hatred being completely dispelled and instantly replaced by an immaculate and luminous sky.

I'm going to tell you two Tibetan stories, principally concerning anger, which show how this alchemy of emotions can operate.

The Story from His Holiness the Twelfth Gyalwang Drukpa

His Holiness the Twelfth Gyalwang Drukpa one day told us the story of one of his predecessors who had chosen as his student a giant monk, a boorish man, well over six feet tall, who made a big impression on everyone. This monk radiated nothing but aggression, but his lama had nevertheless chosen him as a disciple, although those around him had advised against it. This student was ready to give up his own life in order to protect and serve his master.

One day bandits attacked them. Even though his lama had inculcated him with ideas of compassion and nonduality, the student had not yet attained enlightenment. On this occasion, the lama ordered him to do nothing, to take no action, and to say nothing, and the lama handed over everything he had to the bandits. Finding this a bit strange, the leader of the bandits thought that the lama was hiding something more valuable on his person, so he angrily grabbed the lama, intending to shake him up. At this, the disciple became mad with rage and was consumed by intense anger. He picked up the bandit with one hand and was about to take his life. Just then the master shouted, "No!" and at this the disciple fainted and fell to the ground, stiff as a board, releasing the bandit. At the sight of this marvel, that a tiny lama could overcome such a giant—even though he was his student—with a single sound nailing him to the ground, the bandits were so frightened that they left all the lama's goods and ran away howling with fright.

His Holiness the Twelfth Gyalwang Drukpa Rinpoche said that according to the story, when the disciple awoke he had attained Awakening and had enormous compassion for all beings.

☯ The Story from His Eminence Gangten Tulku Rinpoche

Another Tibetan story, related by His Eminence Ganten Tulku Rinpoche, also shows how anger erupting with incredible fierceness increases tenfold the power and brilliance of the strength of wisdom.

In Tibet, a monk left his village and went to a great master in order to practice the dharma. All those close to him having been killed—his father, his mother, and the rest of his family—he had taken the vows of a monk and practiced assiduously with this master for several years.

One day, while he was carrying out some task his master had set him, a man approached him, made three prostrations before him, and asked him for a blessing that is carried out by a placing of hands on the head. At that moment the monk recognized his worst enemy. Falling into terrible anger, he grabbed a long knife, able to think of nothing but exterminating this enemy who had killed his father, his mother, his whole family.

In the grip of this incredibly intense anger, he leapt on this man to take his life, but upon seeing this, the man took flight. The monk pursued his enemy and, just as he was about to cross the threshold of the monastery door, his master called him by his monk's name and said, "Wait a moment! Listen!"

As the monk turned around he added, "Who is angry? See its essence! Look!"

His Eminence Ganteng Tulku Rinpoche makes clear that as the monk was brandishing the knife, he instantly recognized the intrinsic essence of his anger as being mirrorlike wisdom.

☯ Without Beginning, without Permanence, without End

Since all individuals in their present situations are incapable of grasping and understanding the indestructible reality of the mind, one might wonder how the teaching of Sengueï Ngaro views the practitioner's progression toward fewer mistakes and less aggression.

It is true that the inability to grasp the natural and ultimate reality, called *shunyata,* condemns beings to continue to make mistakes. The imperfections persist and one must consider the mind as a field of investigation in which to discover a nature, an essence, and various attributes.

One of these investigations will lead to the realization that the mind is without beginning, without permanence, and without end, and that moment by moment it undergoes change and disintegration. This is fundamental to the practice of the martial art because it also applies to gesture: such movement must not be conditional.

☯ The Noncompound

Acting in such a way that various movements are not conditional means that they must not depend on one another. This is related to the Buddhist teaching of compound, or conditional, existences: *dudjé* (*dus byas*). Such existences are characterized by a birth, a duration, and an end. As such, they are conditional and depend on one another: everything that is born must die, everything that is raised up will be lowered, and everything that is reunited will one day be separated.

The art of Sengueï Ngaro seeks to find the noncompound *dü ma je* (*dus ma byas*), rather than compound existences. This kind of acting— or reacting—is then non-conditioned.

Gesture must be empty, not born. It must be ungraspable, impermanent, without coming and going. The movement is there, but if we try to observe it, we don't see it. If we look for it, we can't find it. Nevertheless it remains, but is not at rest. In coming to see absolute nature, we sever the root of illusion—the illusion of an attacker, someone attacked, and an attack.

Therefore: no aggressor, no person aggrieved, and no aggression. The situation of aggressiveness disappears as well, since nothing escapes disintegration.

All things that are compound are destined to disintegrate, since the experience and knowledge of what we conceptualize as being aggression are impermanent, and therefore subject to disintegration. Moment by moment, the mind undergoes this disintegration. Nothing is constant or eternal.

Here there is a key teaching that is very useful for the practice of meditation under tall waterfalls of icy water and equally suitable for other conditions as well. Indeed, the cascade has no beginning, no permanence, and no end. The cascade comes from a stream, which itself arises from rainfall, which itself comes from clouds that themselves are fed by the evaporation of water from the sea, and so on. One can then say that the cascade has no point of origin. The cascade itself has no permanence since it is disintegrating at every moment in its ongoing flow. The cascade also has no end, since it flows into the water of the lake with which it has just merged.

When a situation of aggressiveness comes up, whatever it may be, I invite you to question yourself about its point of origin, its permanence, and its end.

☯ The Natural State of Being

Being free of the duality of a subject that attacks and an object that is attacked allows the consciousness to root in a natural state of being. By recognizing the evidence of the fading away of all phenomena, you root yourself in the vision of the "great perfection," the Dzogpa Tchenpo, which transcends the intellect. Bringing that into being does not necessarily require years of practice. However, it does mean training oneself right from the beginning to create nothing and change nothing within this momentary consciousness of the present, where the past has ended and the future has not yet been set in motion.

That's how this process unfolds during an act of aggression. Normally, the intellect bursts forth armed with various measures designed to thwart the attack. The person who is the object of aggression will not see the appearances as being transparent and empty, as if they were illusory, or dreamlike, apparitions. In contrast, the practitioner of Sengueï Ngaro will find his consciousness in a free state of the temporal dimension in which past thoughts have died away and thoughts to come have not yet arisen.

☯ Without Center or Periphery

When an aggressor appears in front of you and is going to hit you within a quarter of a second, how can this way of seeing things as an illusion, or a "dreamlike apparition," help you react in a way that is adequate and error-free?

In fact, by rooting your consciousness in a state of emptiness that is not ruled by the situation and is free of all intellectualization, you can come to a state of calm that is like empty space, stripped of effort and free of extremes. You need to be without center or periphery. At such a moment, even though objects rise up before your six senses—the sound of weapons, the sight of the aggressor, and so on—you need to allow your consciousness to come to the light on its own. The aggression will be self-liberated, and thoughts will evaporate without a trace, like waves in water. My master said, "A lama warrior leaves no burning trail in the sand."

That means that there is no point of origin, not a trace of steps that would indicate provenance, no resting place, no precise direction indicating a movement from the center to the periphery, and no cessation—no termination of footprints in the sand. In the application of the martial art of Senguëï Ngaro, this principle is fundamental.

But this means that a lama warrior must act outside of the extreme perspectives of permanence and annihilation. Even though he walks on the sand, his footsteps leave no trace. Being focused on emptiness, he cannot become mired in the sand of illusion.

☯ Concentration on Emptiness

But how does one come to emptiness? It can sometimes require long periods of meditation. Besides, such periods can be used to consider phenomena as if they were a dream, and through that to clarify the mode of the ego's grasping. By realizing how your limited perception of phenomena is not the sole means of experiencing the appearances of the phenomenal world, your vision will show you the misleading character of your present mode of perception. Little by little you will develop a meditative state similar to empty space, and perceive the true mode of existence.

Other forms of meditation are intended to direct the practitioner's introspection toward emptiness itself. There are also methods designed to maintain a concentration on emptiness. However, in that case you need to already have a clear idea of emptiness so that you don't go astray.

It is said that trying to come to emptiness is like walking along a very narrow path that is strewn with obstacles and traps and lined on each side with high snowbanks. In order to avoid tumbling into the deep snowbank of this image and getting bogged down, and to arrive safely at your destination, it is vital to develop concentration and watchfulness at each step. If you don't want to go astray or take the wrong path, you have to avoid extreme views of permanence and annihilation. The first step consists in believing in the clinging to self and phenomena. The second step consists in realizing conclusively that everything is nonexistent. My teacher Lama Tra, especially during certain practices of Yoga Tchouzar, showed me different methods for concentrating on emptiness. One such method uses six examples to assist the meditator in maintaining a concentration on emptiness:

- The mind must be luminous and vigilant, just as the sun illuminates a whole country at one moment with its brilliance. There is no shadow or dullness, and the mind shines with this luminous knowledge called *rigpa*. Ignorance, called in Tibetan *marigpa*, or darkness, and very much related to dream or illusion, will no longer seep into your relations with all things as it is accustomed to doing. Instead, the sunlight of rigpa will bring the true manner of existence of phenomena into the light. This shining light spreading out in all directions symbolizes that one is now able to perceive clearly the two levels of existence: conventional and absolute.
- The mind must be calm and free of agitation like the depths of a vast ocean. As opposed to the waterfall that is constantly agi-

tated and tumultuous, the mind must remain serene. No matter what is encountered, each situation must be used in a way that expands the spirit of Awakening. As a burning torch brightens when dowsed with oil, each situation, even the most conflict ridden, will strengthen the burning flame of the spirit of Awakening and support an uninterrupted journey along the path.

- The mind needs to be like that of a young child staring wide-eyed at temple frescoes. Like a mirror that reflects appearances without modifying them, the mind remains absorbed in emptiness and does not distinguish what is beautiful or ugly, peaceful or wrathful. The mind contemplates emptiness through the eye of knowledge without trying to distinguish details or deep qualities.

- The mind must be like a soaring *garuda* very high up in the sky. By remaining immersed in the space of emptiness, it is possible to have, with very little effort, a panoramic view without needing to analyze the details. Like the garuda, which beats its wings from time to time, this avoids sleepiness and creeping exhaustion. If you don't apply yourself with enthusiasm, perseverance, and zeal, your meditation on emptiness will sink into dullness and you will soon find yourself on the ground.

- Like a pigeon following a ship on the open seas, the mind must overcome thoughts that disturb meditation. The pigeon strays only a certain distance from the ship before realizing the immensity of the ocean, and returning very quickly to its point of departure. Similarly, if the thoughts arising in your mind do not have importance attached to them, when you observe how they arise, remain, and then disappear, the thoughts diminish and you naturally return to the object of your meditation: emptiness.

By watching over the doorways of the body, of speaking, and of the mind, you develop vigilance and attention. When the mind wanders after thoughts that are foreign to meditation or are non-virtuous, it is this attention, like a steel hook, that takes hold of the mind and leads it back to the right position.

- However, when this last method turns out to be inadequate, it's necessary to use another in order to overcome dispersion and dissatisfaction, or various wanderings of a mind stimulated by desire, aggressiveness, and various emotions. The mind must be like a strong, sharp blade that sharpens the arrows of a skillful archer.

In the same way that a sword directly cuts through a volley of arrows, the mind must ceaselessly develop intense concentration in order to avoid being wounded by disturbing emotions. For this to take place, the person meditating must generate flawless vigilance and perfect self-mastery.

The strength behind this sword is not its double edge or the brilliance of its blade, symbols of the emptiness and clarity of the mind, but in the motivation of the person wielding it. He must above all act with compassion and with love. Becoming discouraged in the face of adversity or the ill will of certain people will only weaken the spirit of Awakening. Therefore, you must not let yourself be affected by your surroundings, and at every moment you must maintain an altruistic wish for complete realization that will benefit all beings.

PART THREE

The Practice of
Sengueï Ngaro

CHAPTER FIVE

THE PROFOUND TECHNIQUES OF SENGUEÏ NGARO

THE POSTURES OF STANDING MEDITATION

The first martial arts techniques to be learned when beginning the practice of Sengueï Ngaro are the Window of the Sun (in Tibetan, *Nyimaï gyégong*) and three "forms of standing meditation." All three are unique to Sengueï Ngaro. They consist of three separate postures that are also called "standing meditation postures of the lama warriors." In fact, the lama warriors regularly used these postures to meditate, but also to conserve and circulate vital energy in the center of the body, at a single point, exactly four finger-widths below the navel.

By focusing on an exact point it is possible to increase the quantity and intensity of energy. This allows a better flow of energy through the body when the energy needs to be called upon to carry out martial arts techniques. If you manage to practice this kind of standing meditation posture in a regular way, concentrating on the energy points of the body, you can draw a maximum amount of benefit from this practice.

It is necessary, however, to respect certain essential factors if you wish to stimulate the awakening of energy and promote its free circulation through the body. In order for this practice to be beneficial, certain precautions must be taken. These can be summarized in five essential points:

- First of all, select a suitable location. The practice site must be chosen with foresight. It needs to be peaceful so that you do not risk being disturbed or distracted.

- Next, choose a practice time. This depends on your free time, but the ideal time is between midnight and noon. You can also train very early in the morning, for instance, before going to work. Regardless of the hour you are able to practice, it will always be beneficial, but it is important to repeat these postures with regularity, as close as possible to the same time every day.

- Then, there is the proper posture of the body. The first two postures use "the horseback posture"—in Tibetan, *Zonpeï namgyur*—the legs parallel. The third is "the dragon posture," with the legs crossed. The back must be very straight, without stiffness or tension. This way the energy can circulate freely. The feet must be planted firmly on the ground and the head must remain aligned with the pelvis and the spine. These particular postures are certainly uncomfortable for a beginner, and this type of exercise can seem boring and useless. However, if you practice assiduously and persevere, you will find extraordinary richness in this exercise. These postures were designed to control the senses, stimulating and facilitating the entry of vital energy, always bringing it back below the navel with each breath.

- The fourth point has to do with correct breathing. After breathing in naturally, without forcing, hold all of the breath below the navel. Then let it go gradually as you exhale, without losing your concentration on the energy point being used. As you finish breathing out, completely empty the lungs, very strongly, then hold with all the breath out. Some people can have difficulty in concentrating on a single point while holding and letting go of the breath or while carrying out the movements. It is very important not to continue the holding of energy for too long. If you accumulate excessive energy, it can lead to difficulty with breathing and other physical problems. Therefore, you must not hold the posture or the breath for too long.

- The last point consists in maintaining the right concentration. This involves both the movement of energy and holding it on a point. First of all, you need to be watchful in following the movement of energy in the body. The first standing posture, for example, mainly alternates the circulation of energy in one arm and then the other. This posture is, by the way, a preparation for the sequence of the form of eight short movements and eight long movements. In this particular posture, it is important to avoid any excessive accumulation of energy along the spine. Only the fists must be clenched firmly; the rest of the body must remain totally relaxed.

Even though advanced practitioners can execute these postures and hold them for more than two hours, just a few abdominal breaths carried out correctly are sufficient to bring the energy to the navel.

THE EIGHT SHORT MOVEMENTS AND THE EIGHT LONG MOVEMENTS

This form, which is very short, is the foundation of all the techniques and martial arts forms of Sengueï Ngaro. The form of eighty-six movements, as well as that of the forty-two Buddha palms and the ten techniques of Dun dro tchou, are derivative and are only specific applications of the technique of the eight short movements and the eight long movements. (See plate 20.)

This practice uses a specific breathing technique and calls on a complete utilization of one's energy when doing the movements. It is used as preparation before any session of Sengueï Ngaro, and precedes carrying out the sequence of any particular "form" (in Tibetan, *zug*). It alternates a short strike with a long one, and uses both arms and legs without changing the standing position, except in the long circular strike. The difference between a short movement and a long movement is twelve to eighteen inches, depending on the practitioner's flexibility and body type.

This technique is based essentially on rapidity and precision in hitting the target of the strike, as well as in returning to start position. This allows you to avoid being held, or even to counter with a sequence of movements in different directions without changing your footing.

This form is unique to Sengueï Ngaro. It is not a boxing technique because it is not used the same way in a conflict as in the practice of the form itself. In an actual conflict the fist never remains closed, and it is usually with an open palm that you will touch sensitive areas in your counter moves.

The form of eight short movements and eight long movements is simply an exercise for developing speed, strength, and concentration. This basic practice also coordinates movement, breathing, and the mind.

It is practiced with slow movements, concentrating the breathing on each movement, then speeding up the sequence to increase strength. If the practitioner doesn't manage to coordinate his breathing with his gestures and his mind, he won't make progress in this kind of exercise and he will get no benefit from it. He will be quick, but the quickness will go only so far; he soon will be out of breath and his strength will decrease.

The art of Sengueï Ngaro is based on this quickness, and the speed itself depends on concentration, so a practitioner's quickness can be evaluated with this kind of exercise. Some advanced students can execute ten movements in the time it takes others to execute three. Other exercises test the force of impact when a blow is struck, or check concentration by placing various targets in one's vicinity at certain times.

The essence of this form is to foster complete watchfulness in the senses, and to develop the perceptions of the six senses.*

THE FORM OF EIGHTY-SIX MOVEMENTS

This form goes back to the founder of Senguëi Ngaro, Lama Daidot. It is, therefore, very old and especially valuable. Transmitted without interruption through a lineage of lama warriors of Senguëi Ngaro, it has not once been modified in nine generations. (See plates 15, 16, 17.)

All other techniques have been derived from this particular form, notably the form of the ten animals. Their addition has completed and enriched the original form.

According to legend, some of these movements were transmitted by masters from the realm of Shambhala to a hermit who then transmitted them to Lama Daidot. This form is very secret, since it is at the root of the art of Senguëi Ngaro. All the various martial arts forms were developed from this original form.

The eighty-six movements are like an alphabet. Each movement is a letter, and each letter has a sound and a meaning. Knowing how to string together these eighty-six movements is like constructing phrases. But the most difficult part to learn is the grammar.

This means that certain movements cannot be strung together without respecting certain rules. Just as a verb can't be placed before its subject, it would not be right to execute a counterblow without first having engaged in a feint and parry.

However, the most important point in Senguëi Ngaro is not *learning* the language but the use you make of the language. Some students become writers, others poets, and others playwrights. Some practice law,

---

*Sight, hearing, smell, taste, touch, and intellectual conceptualization.

others philosophy. Once you have learned Sengueï Ngaro, you must use it in the right way so that it is as useful as possible to others. You may enrich or adapt it, but you may in no way modify it by changing its nature and essence.

These eighty-six movements and how they relate to one another cannot be entirely explained, nor can they be analyzed into components in a book. These are not gymnastic sequences or a kind of meditation in movement that can be broken down and illustrated with pictures and explanations.

Someone who wants to practice this form regularly has to have received the teaching and the explanation of each movement from a teacher who has practiced and mastered the form himself. After becoming experienced in it, he will be able to realize the meaning of this practice and discover for himself the many benefits of what Sengueï Ngaro really is.

It would be almost impossible to describe in a single book all the physical and therapeutic benefits of each movement, or even the way that circulation is stimulated among these three systems: the internal organs, the energies that are called *loung* in Tibetan, and the blood. Similarly, it would be foolish to try to describe each movement, or to try to explain precisely the subtle link among different ways of executing the same movement and its different martial arts applications, each one of which is linked to a particular way of breathing.

It can be very challenging to think that the mysterious origin of Sengueï Ngaro and the fact that it comes from a fabled kingdom like Shambhala could, in itself, bring benefits to its practice.

Many stories have been spun about the kingdom of Shambhala, so many people think of it as a paradise where everything is experienced as marvelous and delightful.

The Venerable Bokar Rinpoche has clarified this as follows: "Many people would perhaps be quite disappointed if they went to live in Shambhala, where of course there are no televisions, no entertainment, no pleasant diversions, and so on. It could be rather unpleasant, and a source of confusion or tension. The reality of this kingdom is not necessarily what you envision."*

Certain individuals will not necessarily take pleasure in practicing these eighty-six movements, and may even find them difficult and tiring. Even if these movements come from Shambhala, it may be that after practicing them once, you will never again wish to hear of this Tibetan martial art.

You might think, then, that these eighty-six movements are not a practice that is easy to learn and master. In fact, the apprenticeship has two aspects: one is linked to motivation and the other to the specificity of Sengueï Ngaro.

Right from the start, the eighty-six movements of the lama warriors require strong motivation. Then you must generate transcendent perfections, especially patience, effort, and concentration. If you have these virtues and cultivate them throughout your practice, you will be able to reap the benefit: the perfection of wisdom. There will no longer be problems because nothing will seem difficult or easy.

Second, the practice of these eighty-six movements actually contains all the essential techniques for bringing the energies of the body, the breathing, and the mind into relationship with the entire environment.

This is really a huge task to accomplish right at the beginning. In most traditional martial arts, very often one begins with simple forms† and then moves on gradually to more complex and technical forms.

In Sengueï Ngaro it's the opposite. Right from the beginning you work with the nature of the mind. Instead of becoming attached to working with the exterior form, you essentially work to control the breathing that unifies mastery of gesture and the forms with contemplation of the mind and emptiness.

The mastery of the practice of the eighty-six movements comes through the various oral teachings, which the teacher reveals to the

---

*Oral teaching given before the Kalachakra initiation at Panillo in Spain.
†In Japanese, Kata, and in Chinese, Tao.

student throughout his apprenticeship. The student himself must discover the meaning of each movement and adapt it to each moment, relative to his own capabilities, so that he can maximize his strength and concentration. This form often uses movements in a spiral, called *méri yogul,* like in the masked dances of the Lama. The term *méri* furthermore points out in the traditional thangkas painting of spirals formed by the flames of angry divinities. These spirals, therefore, essentially resemble the development of the internal heat and diamond-hard wrath.

There is, by the way, a distinctive indication that shows whether or not the student has mastered the whole series of these eighty-six movements. I'm speaking about the salutation gesture that is specific to lama warriors. This gesture is the last of the sequence of eighty-six movements. If a student makes a salutation in this way, it shows that he has mastered this form completely, and that he has received all the explanations and commentaries. The way the practitioner carries out this salutation determines his membership in the school of Sengueï Ngaro, and indicates the level of his practice.

THE FORM OF THE FORTY-TWO PALMS OF THE BUDDHA

The form of the forty-two palms of the Buddha, called *Sangye thelmo cheunyi,* is executed very slowly, by pushing with the open palms of the hands using several gestures and in several different directions. (See plates 18 and 19.)

This very ancient technique can be carried out several times, and any individual, regardless of his strength, age, or even his state of health, can practice this exercise. It can be carried out at any time and, if possible, outdoors in a natural environment. It focuses essentially on slowness and on meditation in movement. In this way, the slow gestures, which are not tiring, follow one another without loss of energy.

The movements of stretching and flexing—in fact, all the positions the body assumes—require no extraordinary physical capabilities. On the contrary, as Lama Tra put it, "Every person must work with his own body, his own tensions, and his own capabilities. Don't imitate me. Look for harmony in yourself. By working in this way, neither weakness nor strength will overtake you.

This exercise is specifically recommended before beginning a more in-depth training with Sengueï Ngaro, because it lessens tension, anger, and anticipation. It leads to a deep relaxation of the body combined with an extreme concentration of the mind.

In the form of the forty-two palms of the Buddha, the mind must not start wandering. The movements lead from one into the next as naturally as possible, which assists the coordination of mind, body, and breathing.

Because of this triple coordination, the practice of this form gradually fosters a powerful and harmonious functioning of one's energy. In this exercise the energy is channeled so that it can be emitted from the palms of the hands.

Breathing is central to this particular form. In order to breathe correctly, it is especially important to learn to master abdominal breathing, called *tummo,* which combines meditation and physical heat.

Ordinarily we breathe very poorly: it's too fast, or it's choppy, or it doesn't use the lower part of the lungs. If you manage to master correct breathing, you can economize a large proportion of your energy whether you're standing, seated, walking, or even lying down. There is a very close connection between correctly executed posture and breathing during the execution of this posture without inhibiting energy flow.

The form of the forty-two palms of the Buddha fosters great inner well-being and removes fatigue and agitation. If, for example, you get up in the morning very tired and haven't had enough sleep, there is a certain way of doing this exercise with a breathing and a rhythm that are slightly different. Doing this will bring you extra energy and the fatigue will immediately disappear.

If, on the other hand, you have been buffeted around in your activities and have developed stress and useless tension, there is also a particular breathing in which you can engage. This breathing, slightly different from the previous one, is based on a rhythm designed to control the flow of randomly circulating, uncontrolled energy. It emphasizes the stopping, and alternates full and empty. By doing this, the flow of energy returns to equilibrium. Lama Tra often recommended, "Whatever is tense must relax, and whatever is too relaxed must be energized."

Full and empty is the beat of the universe. Light banishes darkness and darkness swallows light. In the form of the forty-two palms of the Buddha, certain movements are done so as to completely remove muscular tension from one side of the body while the other side is held in maximum tension.

Through this cycle of breathing combined with very slow movement, we become capable of carrying out, as in the case of the secret forms of the animals or in a combat situation, a complete series of martial arts techniques at lightning speed and with maximum intensity. And we do this without losing any vitality or being out of breath. It's really surprising! But the essential thing is this specific breathing, which is at the heart of the alternation of full and empty.

The last gesture, which is called "picking up the flower," allows a total transfer of bodily energy from the tips of the toes to the tips of the fingers of the open palm. This movement completes the series of forty-two movements and completes the circulation of energy in the whole organism. (See plate 18.)

THE SONG OF THE LOTUS ROSARY

The form of the forty-two palms of the Buddha essentially helps avoid dispersing the flow of energy circulating in the body. This energy must be concentrated and directed into the various movements.

The goal of this practice is to not lose the subtle union between mind and movement. The student strives to activate this energy by filling all the parts of the body with it, and by adopting essential principles such as the alternating of full and empty, continuity and change, heaviness and lightness, and so on.

If you don't practice, you might misunderstand the exact meaning of these principles. Nevertheless, I'm going to give you a short and direct explanation that sums up the essence of the secret principles of the form of the forty-two palms of the Buddha. I have put this teaching into the form of a song.*

All these principles are spelled out in The Song of the Lotus Rosary. Here we describe the way in which the movements, the mind, and the breathing must be set in motion so that they are rhythmic and harmonious. The form of the forty-two palms of the Buddha must be carried out as if you were moving through the beads of a rosary. Here is what the song has to say:

> *Eh ma ho!*†
> *Tell one by one*
> *The beads of the lotus rosary,*
> *Not too big, not too small,*
> *Not too crowded together, not too spaced apart:*
> *Without beginning, without end.*
>
> *In movement, be motionless*
> *Like the water of a cascade that turns to ice;*
> *And, motionless, be in movement*
> *Like ice melting in the water of a lake:*
> *Without accumulation, without dispersion.*

---

*This song reveals the essence of the forty-two palms of the Buddha and contains several secret principles transmitted orally by Lama Tra. It has been extracted from the teaching collection *La Cascade des Chants Vajra* (The Cascade of Vagra Songs).
†*Eh ma ho* means "What a great joy!"

Breathe in, bending the bow of nonchange
Like the tiger ready to bound from his lair;
Breathe out, releasing the arrow of concentration
Like a white garuda sweeping down on the naga:
Without balance, without imbalance.

Distinguish what is essential from what is not
Like the roaring of the lion from the mountain silence;
Neither short movement, nor long movement,
Alternate between full and empty through opening and
  closing:
Without exterior, without interior.

Unify visible and invisible, steel and cotton,
And, through extreme gentleness, achieve extreme force;
Neither hard, nor soft, ride the energy of heaven,
Like the dragon in clouds gilded with the dawn:
Without folding in, without moving out.

THE FORM OF THE FISHERMAN LAMA

There is also a martial arts form that is done with a long staff. This form carries the name "fisherman lama." This name has been transmitted in the oral tradition of Sengueï Ngaro. Lama Tra told me a story about this form that uses the long staff. He had received it from his teacher and told it to me during my apprenticeship in the first movements. The technique of the staff, which is called in Tibetan *Khor wa*, is truly effective in an awesome way.

A long time ago, a lama warrior who was an advanced practitioner in the art of Sengueï Ngaro was in the midst of fishing when he was attacked by a wild animal that leapt onto his back. The lama was in a horseman's stance and had a firm grip on the long pole in his hands, which he held above his head. He was motionless, ready to capture the fish that had just swallowed the bait he had carefully positioned on the surface of the water. Surprised by the sudden attack of the leaping animal and having his hands engaged in holding the rod above his head, he turned around spontaneously and with a natural circling movement of the arms he immediately stopped the animal's attack with a single blow.

By combining swiftness, concentration, and force in this circular movement of the rod, he created the first technique of the long staff in Sengueï Ngaro. Realizing the effectiveness of this type of movement, the lama subsequently developed this form of the long staff, which today comprises eighty-six movements and is called "fisherman lama" (in Tibetan, *Lama ngapa*).

According to Lama Tra, this form has remained unchanged since its creation; it still has the complete series of eighty-six movements that are done in a continuous sequence with the long staff. Combined with foot movements specific to Sengueï Ngaro, notably rotation, this form is unique to the style of the lama warriors.

The last movement of the long staff technique relates to the origin of this practice and is based on one of the postures of standing meditation. This posture is called "fisherman lama." At this moment, you hit the ground very quickly with the staff and return to an on-guard position with the staff pointing at the sky. This gesture completes the sequence of the long staff techniques. The ending pays homage to its originator, and is a reminder of the considerable energy that can be developed in this simple posture and by this gesture alone.

This style includes numerous techniques of defense and counterattack, blocking and disarming, and slashing and striking. Many of these moves are unique to the style of the fisherman lama. They cannot be found in traditional Chinese or Japanese* schools of martial arts, even though these schools include elaborate use of the long staff.

---

*In particular, Japanese Bojutsu.

There are several important points about the long staff and how it is handled:

- First of all, the length of the staff is calculated according to two factors: the person's height and the distance from one hand to the other when the arms are extended out to the sides. The difference between these two measurements should not be more than four inches, according to each person's body type.
- The staff is chosen by its length. Traditionally fashioned of very light bamboo, it should be made up of ten knots and ten sections, so that you can get the precise correct length.
- In handling the staff, there are special points to be made about how to hold it and the kinds of movements to be made with it, in movements and in warm-up.
- The staff can be held with one hand, two hands, or no hands. Most commonly it is held with two hands, as one would hold a sword. Speaking of this particular hold, Lama Tra said, "One hand is connected to firmness and stillness and the other to lightness and mobility."
- The first hand, which is placed at the bottom of the staff—closest to the body—is connected to emptiness; and the second hand— placed at the top of the staff—is associated with active compassion directed toward the ten directions of space.
- The staff is thus the extension of the mind and of the body at the same time. When the staff, the mind, and the body become completely one, then you have truly begun to enter into the practice of the long staff.
- It's possible also to observe the rapid transition from very simple but dreadfully effective movements to more-complex movements that sometimes combine a feint with stunning acrobatics.
- The connecting threads between these types of movements are concentration, continuity, and speed. Certain exercises with the long staff are designed to enhance these three virtues.

- There is another noteworthy feature of the style of the fisherman lama: spiral transfers of the arms combined with circular feints with the legs. Unique to Sengueï Ngaro, the two are combined in order to develop a greater than normal striking force and very quick and unstoppable counterblows.
- The salutation gesture itself is unique to Sengueï Ngaro. It is done in the same way as the secret techniques of the ten animals. This salutation is executed in three planes: vertical, horizontal, and sagittal,* with the staff held in the right hand.
- The form of the fisherman lama also combines numerous techniques in space and in time. This allows one to more rapidly anticipate an attack and to feint, while at the same time adapting the counterattack to the distance between one or more opponents and oneself.

In the first case, in the movement "the rolling up of the serpent," the staff is not held in the hands, even when it is moved from the right side to the left side. In this movement the staff is held only in the hollow of the elbow and is anchored against the back. The movement is executed through 180 degrees in the form, but in a combat situation can be done in less or can even move through 360 degrees, depending on your position in relation to the opponent. Even though it is done without the hands, this movement is particularly effective and its power is increased tenfold by using the rotation of the hips and the anchoring of the staff against the back.

It is also found in the movement called the "branch falling to the ground." In this technique, the beginning of the movement takes place by dropping the staff, which falls to the ground as if it had slipped away involuntarily. However, the other end of the staff remains balanced on the palm of one hand, extended open to the sky.

---

*[For a good picture of these three planes, look toward the bottom of the article at http://en.wikipedia.org/wiki/anatomical_terms_of_location. —*Trans.*]

At just this moment, the opponent thinks he can move into assault and launch unopposed a free and clear attack. Then you relaunch the staff very quickly, making it twirl in place without holding on to it with the hands. Once the staff has been caught in flight, you execute a short-strike counterattack by very quickly cutting downward or diagonally. The effect is surprising because the opponent is not expecting it at all!

There are eight specific exercises in all that are part of the art of the staff and support the development of concentration, continuity, and speed. One of these is done in near darkness or in the middle of the night. Four candles are placed at the four cardinal compass points and using cutting or circular movements you must extinguish only their flames, stopping the staff a few inches from the candles without touching them. You begin with one candle, then once the concentration has been established you try to maintain it with other targets placed in various positions in the space.

By doing this, you develop continuity. Once you can move from one target to another without losing energy or speed, you begin to develop force. This doesn't mean physical force; rather, it means the force of concentration of your mind.

Certain exercises are very simple whereas others require acrobatic movement. Just because we speak of simple techniques doesn't mean that they are necessarily easy or ineffectual. It is also incorrect to think that when we label techniques as complex or requiring acrobatic movement, we automatically mean they involve difficulty and feats of physical strength.

During my training with the long staff, Lama Tra always reminded me of a teaching of his master, Lama Bui:

> *For a movement that's easy to learn:*
> *One thousand repetitions are needed to understand it.*
> *For a movement that's complicated to understand:*
> *One single execution is needed to learn it.*

This means that studying a simple gesture and memorizing it is not enough to fully understand its effectiveness and know how to use it correctly in an aggressive situation. Very often, it must be repeated several times so that you can better understand it and enter into harmony with that gesture. Each kind of movement must become a part of you.

But this means, too, that by carrying out a gesture simply, even if it's a complicated one, the gesture can immediately reveal a precise teaching. It doesn't matter whether or not you execute it correctly. What counts is to execute it simply. It doesn't matter how complicated the gesture may be: you will understand immediately what it contains, and its richness will instantly appear.

Sengueï Ngaro training often uses one-on-one combat, staff against staff. In fact, this is part of the training with the staff, even though this practice is done with the aim of applying certain specific techniques, rather than falling into a real "free-for-all" combat where you could get hurt. It's important to understand that in Sengueï Ngaro, whether it's with bare hands or with the staff, it's unnecessary to conduct several offensive moves, since the countermove is very often a single move and doesn't require a lengthy exchange. It's not a competition, especially in the art of the staff.

I remember my first training in the long staff with Lama Tra. He came toward me and handed me a long, very light bamboo staff, saying, "I have cut this and prepared it for you. With it you are going to learn and practice the form of the fisherman lama."

Having already practiced with the long staff and being accustomed to using a staff that was rigid and thick, I was quite intrigued as to how effective the bamboo would be. Lama Tra then stood directly in front of me and ordered sharply, "Go ahead. Attack me! Go to it. Be quick and precise."

I was very concerned about my master, who was fifty-nine years old, and even though he, too, was armed with a staff, I was a bit afraid of hurting him. I was greatly surprised when I saw that his countermoves were lightning fast, five times faster than my attacks. His movements were unnerving, and at the same time precise and quick.

You cannot imagine ahead of time all that a practitioner of the fisherman lama style is capable of with a simple bamboo staff in his hand, especially if you haven't practiced this style.

This first confrontation using my staff with Lama Tra ended rather badly. After several desperate attempts to touch him with my staff, and after having received several sharp blows from his counterattacks, I realized that his defense techniques were just as effective as his lightning-fast counterattacks.

The day following this training, I thought I would need a whole series of massage sessions to get back on my feet with training, since besides the blows from his staff, that same day I had to study an entire special warm-up session for the staff that was rather demanding.

Still laughing, Lama Tra said to me, "No need for massage! Stand still, stare at the horizon, and breathe deeply."

He then used one of the applications of medical science of Sengueï Ngaro that he had also mastered. With two fingers, he pressed on two energy points on my back, and after a few seconds, he said, "There we are. Now we can begin the training again!"

Stunned, I realized that I was no longer blocked, and that all my muscle tension had disappeared.

This was one of the applications of the medical science that Sengueï Ngaro had also mastered. Sengueï Ngaro conceals diverse techniques to neutralize an adversary with the activity of certain points of energy: the muscles, the tendons, and, of course, the bones. This technique continues with equal effectiveness with other techniques of "massage" that repace what has been displaced, damaged, or neutralized.

This specific fisherman lama warm-up is made up of a series of eight movements. Each movement is executed for the duration of about ten seconds, all the while holding two staffs, one in each hand, by their ends. The arms are outstretched and are tracing a circular pattern. As you finish, you relax all the muscles, letting the ends of the two staffs fall to the ground and opening the palms of your hands toward the sky. This exercise is very demanding, especially when done a number of times.

This kind of warm-up supports coordination of the body, breathing, and mental concentration on the staff. Two of these movements are done with the staffs crossed, one vertical and the other horizontal, in the on-guard position specific to Sengueï Ngaro. This exercise brings more concentration, strength, balance, and muscle tone.

This kind of technique doesn't require highly developed physical abilities. A young child could very well practice all the techniques of this fisherman lama form, including the warm-up. Like the bamboo itself, which is famous for bending and not breaking, flexibility and strength are derived from working with the long staff. Besides, a good defense is better than a faulty attack.

Flexibility wins out over rigidity. That is why the long staff form is recommended for older people. My teacher, who is no longer in his twenties, practices this art every day. When I would ask him how he was doing, he would always reply, "A session with the long staff in the morning and I'm just fine!" Then he would begin to laugh.

It would be incorrect to think that in order to practice the art of the long staff you have to be an acrobat. On the contrary: the art of the staff helps us to understand how flexibility and strength, movement and stillness, youth and old age complement each other.

There are specific meditations that are done with the staff. Some of these meditations are done standing with the staff in front of you or to the side, holding its end with one or both hands. Others are practiced seated on the ground with the staff pointed to the sky and held in one hand. These meditations, which have a precise aim, foster profound states of concentration.

THE FORM OF THE EIGHT MOVEMENTS THAT EMPTY AND THE EIGHT MOVEMENTS THAT FILL

Also included in the deep techniques are various other forms connected with balancing energy, which can be either excessive or insufficient. The form that addresses this specifically is "the form of eight movements that empty and the eight movements that fill," or, in Tibetan, "Pong Oue Yogul Gyé, Nyam Lèn Yogul Gyé."

This form can be broken down into close to 240 specific movements, all combined in two series of eight specific forms (such as "Nyi Dza Pa," "Shell Ribü Yogul," and "Dordje Thap . . ."). I am not going to develop this vast body of forms in greater detail in this book because it is necessary to provide a much deeper understanding of this teaching in tandem with its practice so that one can grasp all its richness and obtain all the related benefits.

CHAPTER SIX

THE SECRET
TECHNIQUES OF THE
ANIMALS

THE WISDOM OF DUN DRO TCHOU

The practice of Dun dro tchou, which means "ten animals," comprises techniques that are based on the animal kingdom, primarily the ability of certain animals to defend themselves.

This practice affords the possibility of fulfilling your desire to protect beings, and of perfecting your approach to Sengueï Ngaro. The ten techniques are the crane, the tiger, the monkey, the snake, the crab, the bear, the mongoose, the praying mantis, the butterfly, and the dragon.

Certain of these animals—the tiger, for example—usually kill others only when they fight. This is where wisdom enters into the art of Sengueï Ngaro. If you have to respond to a situation of aggression by using the technique of the tiger, that doesn't mean you have to become a tiger and kill your aggressor. A tiger attacks only if it feels attacked, or to feed itself.

If a practitioner possesses the wisdom of Dun dro tchou, his bodhicitta motivation will be reinforced and he will know how to use these various skillful methods correctly and with clarity, in order to help others. Every time you energetically ward off dangers that threaten the lives of others and thereby prevent their being hurt, you learn a little more about how to live a long life. The lama warriors always used these techniques of the animals for defending themselves and for attacking.

The butterfly technique is an example. When the butterfly eludes capture, it is entirely because of the beating of its wings and its skillful use of the air. If it is attacked, it doesn't need to kill its enemy. This is a peaceful and unthreatening creature.

The animals are all different, and according to the particular environment in which they evolved, they can experience various kinds of suffering and react differently to danger. This is why there are exploratory meditations specific to the art of Sengueï Ngaro that allow the practitioner to feel the fear and suffering of the animal kingdom, and to become more and more familiar with certain animals.

There are also three supplementary techniques that are an integral part of Dun dro tchou and are grouped under the name "the spirit of the animals."

THE SPIRIT OF THE ANIMALS

Three of the internal practices specific to Dun dro tchou are the tiger, the mongoose, and the praying mantis. These practices are mainly to assist you in discovering how to work with your natural state. To accomplish this, the form of a movement must be coordinated with a particular breathing and state of mind. This is somewhat close to *Korde rushen** in Dzogchen, since it concerns a strenuous exercise that leads to a state of intense contemplation.

If, for example, a practitioner correctly executes, with total concentration, the thirty-five movements of the spirit of the tiger, he will be able to execute only this form, since it requires intense energy. The

---

*Individual training in Dzogpa Tchenpo being part of the preliminary practices.

precise aim of the exercise is to develop total concentration without becoming hostile or developing the desire to harm others.

Also, if anger is not generated, it's possible to acquire a specific state of clarity that can recognize the luminous nature of the mind. This is why this type of exercise can be compared to the Korde rushen. Through the practice of the three spirits—the tiger, the praying mantis, and the mongoose—you will be able to control the "three doorways": the body, the breathing, and the mind.

The aim is not to become an animal, but rather to develop the wish to never again experience the suffering that animals undergo, and also to make use of your wisdom to transform all of your experiences into spiritual practice. This is why, for example, one doesn't speak of the strength of the tiger, or even of the energy of the tiger, but of the spirit of the tiger.

If you practice these forms correctly, gradually you come to a state of contemplation. This state will become evident before, during, and even more intensely after the execution of this martial arts form.

Arriving at this point, there will no longer be any separation between the world of animals and the world of Buddhas, no longer any difference between a martial arts movement and a state of contemplation. All differences between samsara and nirvana will fade away.

The practice of the spirit of an animal in fact fills two roles: it distances you from external distractions and all obstacles to mental calm; and it bolsters watchfulness, which eliminates internal distractions.

So that the practice of Dun dro tchou is beneficial to beings, and so that you can contemplate the benefits of it, you basically have to keep your body, your breathing, and your mind pure and flawless.

If you don't maintain this purity, your martial art could lead to the action of killing; you will be animated by a strong impulse that impels you to destroy living beings. You will then be no different from an animal.

This is why it is so important to apply the six transcendent virtues during the practice of Sengueï Ngaro. In this way you can face any hostile, dangerous, or uncomfortable situation by abstaining from harming others with bad actions.

Therefore, when you maintain the bodhisattva vows while practicing the art of Dun dro tchou, your actions will become more powerful, thanks to your motivation and self-mastery.

THE FORM OF THE TEN ANIMALS

It would be very difficult to completely describe the ten forms of Dun dro tchou. In fact, to practice all of them would require more than two hours. Also, I can provide only the principal traits that characterize each animal, so that you may be able to understand its nature and its essence.

☯ *The Bear*

The form of the bear is rather short and contains only thirteen movements; in essence, it is based on the feint and using the opponent's force.

This form, called *Dom* in Tibetan, which also uses the movement of the crab, is noted for the use of internal and external rotation of the hip, as well as flexing of the hip. The technique of the bear uses the whole body weight, which helps in developing strength, physical balance, and mental stability.

The movements are solidly anchored to the ground, even though at a given moment you employ a deep bending forward toward the ground with the torso, symbolizing the act of catching a fish in the river. In this precise movement, you throw the arms strongly backward while at the same time making a circular back feint, imitating the catching of a fish in its natural environment. In contrast to the form of the monkey, which uses permanent imbalance, the form of the bear is characterized by an impressive stability.

In the movement just described, its martial arts application is as follows: as your opponent rushes at you head on, the fish being seized by the bear's paws is actually your opponent's foot, which you grab firmly as you skirt by him. The fact of scooping up the fish from its natural environment, the river, means that you are going to cut off anger at its source. The movement of the bear, which pulls violently backward while moving upward at the same time, means that the opponent is going to find himself very quickly thrown into the air. In the end, the opponent is going to find himself in an unaccustomed position, and he's going to wonder very quickly whether or not it's such a good idea to try this ever again!

Of course, in applying this counterattack, it may be that your opponent gets doubly angry and wants to attack again; the anger may not have been entirely uprooted. However, the art of the roaring of the lion was not designed so that, following an attack, you leave it up to the opponent to begin another one, and then another, and so on. That would be falling into the trap of an exhibition or a competition. You must not play with the opponent; you must neutralize him.

A Dzogchen proverb says:

> *When we throw a stone at a dog,*
> *He brings it back to us a thousand times,*
> *But when we throw a stone at a lion,*
> *We only do it once!*

What is the meaning here? The dog sees only the stone and eagerly runs to look for it and bring it back. He can't be distracted from this goal, and his only pleasure is that of the game and of being a little tired. In contrast, the lion immediately sees where the stone is coming from and he certainly doesn't run after it!

This proverb can, in a certain way, be applied to Sengueï Ngaro. For example, if someone attacks you with a weapon despite your having done a great deal to avoid it, you need to cut off this aggressiveness at its root, not by eliminating the weapon or the aggressor, but by eliminating the anger that provoked the attack.

All the techniques of Dun dro tchou must be used only for that. Therefore, it is necessary to counterattack not only with vigilance, concentration, and effectiveness, but above all with the motivation of the spirit of Awakening. The aim is to have the enemy do no more harm— even to become a friend—and to transform an aggressive situation into a situation of peace.

The Tiger

The form of the tiger comprises forty-six movements, which are done very rapidly with the palms open forward and the fingers curled, so that they form a tiger's paw. (See plate 25.) These movements tone the entire system of muscles, tendons, and nerves because they are carried out with complete tension and isometric concentration.

Even if you stop in a posture and several people try to hit you or make you lose your balance, they will not succeed. This form develops considerable energy, both physical and mental.

Most of these movements are intended to unbalance the opponent and knock him down. Depending on the situation and the number of aggressors, certain of these techniques can be used differently: either by practicing simple strikes that hit sensitive or paralyzing areas, by using holds or throws that cause a loss of balance and a fall, or even by pinning the person to the ground.

Only the last movement of this form brings together these three possibilities. It is carried out by blocking an attack; then throwing the opponent off balance, like a tiger bringing the water buffalo to the ground; and by pinning the opponent to the ground. The movement then ends with the tiger's right paw raised while looking up to the sky, the usual sign of victory of the animal over its prey.

⊘ The Mongoose

The form of the mongoose is essentially centered on the animal's agility and the quickness with which it seizes its prey by the neck. Usually, the mongoose rises up on its hind feet with an undulating motion, causing the snake to rise up as well. Then the mongoose seizes the snake in a flash, going directly for its prey without any side moves.

The position of the hands is also unique to the form of the mongoose, and the seizing takes place extremely quickly over short distances, with the aim of bringing the opponent to the ground. (See plate 21.)

This technique combines seizing and ripping away. It is used especially when defending oneself against an opponent armed with a knife or a club. Thus it is used in disarming and can be combined with another technique, such as the butterfly or the tiger.

This form develops breathing capacity and increases concentration and speed.

Seizing is specific to the mongoose. In attacking certain very sensitive areas of the body with precise pressure of the fingers, the bite of the mongoose is paralyzing and lightning fast.

⊘ The Crane

The form of the crane uses a number of broad, circular movements and counters straight-line attacks, whether these come head-on, sideways, or from the rear.

This technique is used to parry and to disarm, but also for blocking and for counterattacks. Many of these movements were inspired by the technique of the short and long circular movements, which themselves were derived from the movements of the crane. (See plates 22 and 23.)

The technique of the crane basically develops a sense of flexibility and agility, but also strengthens the joints of the upper limbs, since numerous circular movements are used.

This form allows you to remain quite distant from your opponent and to counterattack extremely quickly by moving very short or long distances in the briefest space of time and from any direction. The form of the crane is essentially based on defense, as opposed to the form of the mongoose, which concentrates mainly on attack.

⊘ *The Crab*

The form of the crab is the shortest in number of movements. It elaborates a way of moving to the side, diagonally, or backwards, and is basically used for defense.

These twenty-four movements, which can cover short or long distances, combine speed and precision. Once these two factors of time and space are mastered, the practitioner will have improved his ability to feint and to avoid being hit, while at the same time carrying himself in a way that he can counterattack. This technique concentrates on movement of the legs, and doesn't use the arms.

⊘ *The Praying Mantis*

The form of the praying mantis includes several movements that are done by positioning the arms in a way that imitates the front legs of this insect. The praying mantis is called in Tibetan *Seul wa dep bun sin*, which means "the insect that prays," since its two front feet are always raised together as if in prayer.

The praying mantis is a legendary animal with a lightning-fast ability to feint or counterattack.

The strike can be carried out either with the back of the bent wrist or with the points of the fingers—thumb, index finger, and middle finger together. When this technique is used, the feint, parry, and counterattack become a single move. The target strike areas are basically the vital body points, and the intensity of the strike aims to paralyze the opponent's attack.

The first five movements of this form use five specific kinds of movements that allow you to be protected from a strike of any kind, and simultaneously to counterattack. These five particular movements form the actual basis of the technique of the short staff, Khor wa trung thrung, which uses a short staff in each hand.

One of the movements of this form also uses a particular sweeping kind of motion for an attack coming from the rear.

☯ *The Monkey*

The monkey is the form that uses the most acrobatic and supple movements. This technique is based essentially on rolls, quick changes of direction, and certain types of sweeping movements. It fosters your sense of balance and speed, but also allows you to adapt to any changing situation, especially during close-range attacks.

We find one of these techniques in one of the oldest forms of Sengueï Ngaro—the form of the forty-two palms of the Buddha—in which, starting from an on-guard position, you do a roll before curling up into a ball, as a monkey does. This type of roll allows your head to be protected when you fall to the ground, because your arms form a kind of protective ball, but it also acts as a kind of vital feint when you are surrounded by several opponents.

This technique brings together trickery, vice, and agility. None of the movements of the monkey is predictable.

ꕤ The Snake

The form of the serpent uses a hand position that recalls the head of the cobra, and is carried out by combining undulating and circular movements with unpredictable and instantaneous straight-line attacks, striking with the points of the fingers.

Sometimes the counterattack is made alternatively with either the head or the tail of the snake. If it's with the tail, an arm is used to block and parry the attack; the other arm is used to neutralize, either by holds or by very precise strikes to vital points of the body, such as the throat, for example, or even the armpit, which is an especially sensitive area. The form of the snake develops speed, concentration, and suppleness. It has one point in common with the form of the mongoose: even a single one of its attacks can be like a bolt of lightning. The difference between these two forms is that the snake combines hiding with the art of slithering and the mongoose combines the directness of its attacks with the art of rising up when attacking. Notice, however, that it's the mongoose that most often wins out in a confrontation with a snake, regardless of how fearsome the snake is.

ꕤ The Butterfly

The form of the butterfly involves a special position of the arms: the wrists join together and the hands flex very quickly, imitating the butterfly's beating wings.

You might think that using a technique that imitates an insect would be ill-advised when facing aggression from a frightening opponent who is much more powerful than you. But thanks to the movements of the butterfly, you can be capable of handling this kind of situation. This technique also uses counterattacks with the open palm of the Buddha.

Above all, it allows you to feint or block several attacks that come quickly and from different directions without getting hurt. The end of the form combines the blocking technique of the butterfly (for an attack coming from the side) with the counterattack of the crane (using circular long-fist forms).

If this form is practiced correctly, you can acquire speed, precision, and strength. My teacher had me practice this form very often as a warm-up, and he would hold two targets in front of me—one in each hand—moving them constantly. It took a particularly difficult acrobatic move to be able to touch the targets as quickly as possible without losing the basic posture with the wrists joined, which I had to come back to instantly after each strike.

This requires concentration at each moment. You begin with one target and then quickly move on to two targets. Next, the changing position of the targets is accelerated, along with the combination of different counterattacks as they relate to various angles of attack.

☯ *The Dragon*

The form of the dragon uses an on-guard position with the closed fist resting on the palm of the opposite open hand (as in the palm of the Buddha).

The form begins with various blocks—low, middle, and high—while you continue to counterattack with very precise strikes using the feet. The whole of the form of the dragon is centered on techniques using strikes with the feet. Some are done facing the opponent, some at an angle, and some from the side. Other strikes combine different directions or are done in sweeping forms, or even in the form of circular strikes with the feet.

What is characteristic of this technique is the moving of the body like a dragon, by undulating and staying very close to the ground. This form is especially useful when you are faced with several opponents, especially when they are immediately in front of you.

CHAPTER SEVEN

THE ULTIMATE TECHNIQUES OF SENGUEÏ NGARO

THE FORM OF THE FIVE ANIMALS

☯ *The Lung Ta*

The Sengueï Ngaro practice called "the form of the five animals" is related to a very old Tibetan tradition known as *lung ta,* or wind horse. This practice was inspired primarily by the five legendary animals of Tibet: the tiger, snow lioness, garuda, dragon, and wind horse.

These five animals are often represented on the numerous multicolored flags flying near sacred places or temples, or attached to long poles secured on the peaks of Tibetan mountains. This type of flag, which is usually called lung ta, most often carries mantras or invocations intended to continually increase this energy called loung in Tibetan. In fact one of these formulations says:

> *Raise up our life, our virtue,*
> *And our glorious wind horse,*
> *Higher and higher!*

The four corners of Sengueï Ngaro's flag also bear Tibetan inscriptions referring to these animals: *tak* (tiger), *seng* (snow lioness), *khyoung* (garuda), and *druk* (dragon). The central inscription on the flag, indicating the name Sengueï Ngaro, is handwritten in black letters on a blue background. The color blue symbolizes the element of space and the fifth animal, the wind horse. This special Sengueï Ngaro flag is surrounded by several brocade pieces woven with gold thread. A three-pointed flag, it is very similar to the flag usually held by the legendary warrior of Kham, King Ling Gesar, or even that of certain *dharmapalas,* protectors of the lamaist pantheon.

◉ Infusing Strength and Wisdom

Numerous benefits can accrue from the practice of the form of the five animals, for the beginner as well as for the advanced practitioner, young to very old. If you can infuse your body and mind with the strength and wisdom of these animals, you will develop ultimate virtues.

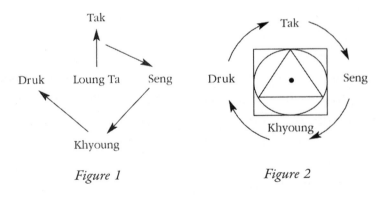

Figure 1   *Figure 2*

This form is quite unique to Sengueï Ngaro. The body is displaced from right to left, which supports the re-creation of the cycle of energy, starting from the center and moving through the four directions of space (fig. 1). These movements may also be done around an axis, a tree, or a *chorten* (fig. 2).

Certain Tibetan chorten, of very old construction, have these four animals painted or sculpted on each of the four sides. What is unique about this form is the sequencing of five types of movement and shifting; they are done in a very specific order. Each movement corresponds to the five elements: earth, water, fire, air, and space.

There is also a fourth kind of movement. It can, incidentally, be done on wooden posts set in a quincunx pattern a few inches or two yards above the ground (fig. 3). This practice on wooden posts is for advanced practitioners, since it combines shifting on the wooden posts with various counterattacks, and strikes with the feet. Some of the exercises are practiced with two people, or in a combat situation. This kind of exercise requires a combination of several faculties: concentration and balance, calm and determination, strength and suppleness. Without such qualities, such a practice would be dangerous, and the risk of falling or getting hurt could be a discouraging factor for beginners. This is not the intention.

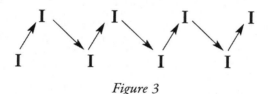

Figure 3

One day while I was training in the execution of this form, in particular the movement of the snow lioness, Lama Tra interrupted me and gave me this valuable advice, which he had received from his own teacher:

> *Move within the purity of the elements.*
> *No tension, no aggressiveness must arise.*
> *Do not battle the snow lioness,*
> *Become the snow lioness,*
> *And through extreme gentleness attain extreme force!*

This advice provides several essential points:

The first insists on this very subtle connection that exists between the five elements and the actual form of the movements: for example, the straight-line movements and the balance shift based on a square for the tiger bounding out of its lair, linked to the element earth. Or the circular movements and the sequence of transfers based on a circle for the snow lioness, linked to the element water. Or also the movements at an angle and the transfers based on a triangle for the garuda casting himself toward the sun, linked to the element fire.

The second point puts the stress on the necessity of dropping all tension and anger in one's movements. Even though each of these five movements is also, in the martial arts pantheon, associated with a parry, a foot strike, or a particular martial arts posture of the hands or feet (see table 1), you need to eliminate tension. Unless you slow down and relax, your approach will be strained or even frantic. Like the tiger, the practitioner must be relaxed and full of energy at the same time. And this energy is, above all, the energy of the spirit of Awakening.

The third point emphasizes how important it is to be inspired by the animals, such as the snow lioness, who moves slowly, gently, and serenely over the snowflakes that carpet her kingdom. This movement allows you to acquire the ability of this animal to judge distances with precision when moving from one point to another or when bounding from one mountain to another. Balance in the execution of movements arises only from bringing together skill and spontaneity. You are not fighting a tiger, nor are you imitating a tiger—you, yourself, are becoming a tiger. The practitioner of Sengueï Ngaro isn't limited to imitating the movements of these animals; he needs to look for something other than slowness and mimicry. He must seek the true, creative forces attributed to each of these mythological animals.*

The last point has to do with the subtle balance that exists between gentleness and strength, and the need to favor gentleness over strength. The more we seek extreme gentleness, the more we will be filled with strength. By combining gentleness and slowness, the mind can remain in a state of calm and concentration. It is important in this to bring

---

*We speak of the "three capabilities" of the snow lioness: miraculous transformations; extreme quickness; and her wings, which fly like the wind.

The Form of the Five Animals

ANIMAL	ELEMENT	ORGAN	GUT	BODY PART	EXTENSION OF BODY PART	DIRECTION	SEASON	DAILY CYCLE	WEATHER	PARRY ON ATTACK	FOOT STRIKE
Tiger	earth	spleen/ pancreas	stomach	muscle	chest/lips	east	late summer	afternoon	wet	in front	in front
Snow Lioness	water	kidney	bladder	bone	hair	north	winter	night	cold	from the side	from the side
Garuda	fire	lung	large intestine	epidermis	breath	west	autumn	evening	dry	from high to low	quarter moon
Dragon	air	heart	small intestine	blood vessels	body hair/ facial color	south	summer	midday	hot	from behind	circular
Lung Ta	space	liver	gall bladder	tissue / brain	nails	center	spring	morning	windy	from low to high	donkey

attention to the breathing, since each movement is connected to a particular way of breathing.* This is why you need to foster balance and neither linger over a movement nor move too quickly on to the next. As soon as you begin this form, it is recommended that you keep a very low center of gravity. This brings in an extraordinary stability and a natural state of watchfulness and attention in the movements.

The general sense of the advice of lama warriors of the past is, then, very simple. The various postures are essentially designed to maintain harmony between mind and body and to establish a state of peace and union of the practitioner with nature and its elements.

☯ Reinforcing Vital Energy

Each movement also has a specific therapeutic property. In fact, each of the animals is connected externally to an element and internally to an organ, a component of the body, or an extension of these components. There is also a strong correspondence with directions in space and with the seasons. Each movement is recommended for a specific period of the year, and ought to be executed in its specific direction in space. (See the table on page 133.)

What connection is there between the therapeutic effect of these five movements and the elements? Based on the form and properties of these five elements (stability, fluidity, mobility, and so on) and the interaction of the energy between the organs and the bowels, this exercise aims at maintaining and reinforcing the vital energy. Since each internal organ is associated with one of the five elements, when the practitioner imitates the characteristic movements of the five animals, he reverses the process of aging and stimulates all functions of the organism. Practicing this form of the five animals rebalances all the vital energies.

And, if you apply yourself to a regular practice of the form of the five animals, you will really be able to experience the coming and going

---

*For the snow lioness, we stress her ability to hold her breath for a long time when traveling through space.

of vital breath, the loung. You will be able to experience it from the marrow of your bones to the surface of the skin, from internal organs to the tips of the fingers, and from your entire being to the edges of the universe. You will also experience a deep state of calm and meditation.

The movements of a specific animal stimulating a specific internal organ, along with the breathing in each balance transfer generating a specific state of meditation, can mean that sometimes you will be quite surprised by this kind of exercise, which, at first glance, may seem simple and easy. Just because a form is done slowly doesn't mean it's easy and relaxing. In fact it is very difficult to combine gentleness and slowness!

There is, by the way, another form that is part of the ultimate techniques of Sengueï Ngaro, called "the form of the ten circles," which also is based on principles of slow movement. The only difference is that the movements of this form of ten circles have no direct martial arts application.

THE FORM OF THE TEN CIRCLES

The form of the ten circles, called in Tibetan *Khor Tchouk,* can be considered as yet another exercise of meditation on the meridians that traverse the body. As it is a true healing art, this form can be practiced only with the aim of regulating and balancing the flow of energy in the organism. As it is a contemplation practice, this practice also supports the coordination of movement, breathing, and the mind. Through it, we will reestablish harmony with the five elements, which are the source of all forms of life in the universe.

These are the essential principles of this particular technique. Just as all forms of life go through birth, growth, accumulation, and disappearance, this cycle of ten movements obeys the law of changes. Each of these movements itself obeys this law of transformation, so that we realize that there is no origination, no continuity, no cessation, no high, no low, no opening, no closing, no center, no periphery, no interior, no exterior.

Through these ten circles, you can penetrate your own depths as you inhale and reach the sun, moon, and stars as you exhale. This coming-and-going movement of energy engenders a state of union with the universe. In completing this form of the ten circles, you can attain the eleventh circle—nothingness!

This form is called the form of the ten circles because it consists mainly of the flowing sequence of ten circular movements that are done in three planes: horizontal, vertical, and sagittal. These ten movements are linked to ten specific breathing patterns, each movement alternating an inhale and an exhale. This cycle of ten breaths is also based on the ten specific circular movements. As for the mind, it is the foundation for the coordination between these ten movements and ten breaths. This coordination is centered basically on the path of the energy along the meridians, in harmony with the surrounding space.

These are the same meridians as those of Chinese acupuncture. The form of the ten circles does use knowledge of the meridians as they are usually described in Chinese acupuncture. But in the art of Sengueï Ngaro, there is a precise knowledge of energy channels other than what is designated under the sphere of meridians. The practitioner has to visualize these meridians and their respective energy points.

Meridians are individual to each person. Chinese sages greatly developed this knowledge, which is known also in Tibetan medicine. Certain of these points are especially useful in the martial art of Sengueï Ngaro, whether it be in caring for others or in paralyzing, putting to sleep, or neutralizing an aggressor by touching just one point.

Learning the meridians and their various points is a requirement in completing the form of the ten circles. Knowing this, you will be able to visualize precisely the circulation of energy throughout the organism and through each vital point as you very slowly perform the ten movements. In each movement the vital energy follows a particular meridian. As the mind rides the breath, you travel along each meridian, one after the other.

The breath is like a horse—a horse of the breath. The mind is the rider and the meridians are the roads. This is a key point in all forms of yoga—each movement corresponds to a particular breath. In each of the ten circles, the energy is governed by a very definite cycle following one particular meridian.

The first five movements of this form allow you to feel right away this powerful flow of energy, beginning or ending at the tip of each finger: first the index finger, then the middle finger, then the ring finger, the little finger, and finally the thumb. The five other movements of the form allow you to follow this energy in various other parts of the body, even to the tips of your toes. The ten circles can be done seated or standing, without using the legs. Only the arms are engaged in these movements.

Visualization is essential for this flow of energy to operate without hindrance. There are numerous instructions connected to these movements, all very simple. A young child or an elderly person can practice them without difficulty. It is possible to feel a deep calm and to come to a state of meditation from the first circle or after a single execution of all ten circles.

However, even though this form seems very easy to memorize and carry out, you actually would need to receive several hours of teaching in order to discover all its secrets, several years of training to experience all its benefits, and perhaps a lifetime of practice to master it.

If you manage to perceive the energy that circulates along these invisible pathways, moving from one energy bridge to another, you will then be able to experience more and more advanced states of contemplation.

However, even if you do not have all the teachings connected to this form, the act of precisely coordinating these movements to their cycle of breathing (breathing in or out) implies that this circulation of energy will take place in any event. From the first practice session you will experience a state of well-being and serenity. It is important that the mind doesn't wander or seek only states of calm and relaxation.

The practice basically supports the development of meditation in movement and contemplation. If you practice this form in a circle with several other practitioners, or carry it out in a sacred place—for example, in a temple, on the top of a mountain, or even on a beach with the rhythm of the waves—you can foster this state of contemplation.

In Sengueï Ngaro, we practice this exercise at the conclusion of training, since it allows us to come back to a deep state of balance where all the participants are recentered on the same energy and rhythm. We practice it three times, each time more slowly.

If you wish, you can do this exercise as many times as you like. It is not tiring and it rebalances the flow of energy. It can even reanimate dormant or seemingly dead nerves.

I'm going to tell you a story about one of my friends, an elderly person whose given name is Maguy. Following a surgical operation to replace one of her cervical vertebrae with a prosthesis, she found herself misaligned on one side compared to the other, from wearing a neck brace for too long. She was unable to look forward without moving her upper torso, and conversely, if her upper torso was facing forward, her head was at a 45-degree angle to the side. Despite all the efforts of doctors and physiotherapists, she seemed condemned to remain like that. If she stretched her arms forward, her fingers were skewed by about six inches. During her first practice of the form of the ten circles, after five or six series, she already had arrived at a certain amount of mobility. After several days of practice on her own, her doctors were amazed to realize that certain nerves that had been declared definitively dead were working again. Their patient had thus regained a great deal of the mobility that she had lost. This is only one example of the many therapeutic properties that are to be found in the form of the ten circles, and the benefits that can sometimes result from its practice.

If you are too relaxed, the form of the ten circles strengthens and brings back alertness. If you are too tense, strained, or stressed, it is calming. When practiced in the morning, this form awakens and stimulates the organism. When done during the day, it maintains wakefulness in the body and mind and avoids deficiencies and excesses of energy. When practiced in the evening, it calms and relaxes tension or fatigue from the day. This is why it's good to practice this form of the ten circles every day, with regularity. It is a jewel left to us by the lama warriors of the past.

PART FOUR

Yoga Tchouzar:
The Essence
of Sengueï Ngaro

CHAPTER EIGHT

THE EXCELLENT TECHNIQUES OF SENGUEÏ NGARO

TCHOU AND KSAR

The excellent techniques of Sengueï Ngaro are called Yoga Tchouzar. This Tibetan expression means a number of things at various levels. At the root of Yoga Tchouzar we find the Tibetan legend of the great goddess of the waters. She springs up from a snow-covered mountain in the form of a beautiful cascade and tumbles into a huge lake. This lake, surrounded by four great rocks, contains all the waters of the world, which extend to the four corners of the earth.

The cascade has the honor of being able to unite so completely with the lake that it is impossible to distinguish the parts of this duo. The amorous conjunction of currents where the waters mix is the symbol of union (*yoga*) and peace (*tchouzar*).

Tchou refers to still waters in Tibetan—those that remain stable and calm, without excessive overflowing; *ksar,* on the other hand, refers to lively water, the leaping up of white, foamy cascades, torrents, waves, or running water.

Yoga Tchouzar can then be translated as "amorous mingling," or perhaps "mixed waters," or even "absolute union."

THE ART OF MIXING THE WATERS

Every practitioner of Sengueï Ngaro must strive to attain the art of Yoga Tchouzar—reuniting two waters that have different natures but the same essence, in peace and through love.

This is not about just the love of one's parents, friends, wife, or children, but the love of all beings, and especially of one's enemies. It means a total, unifying, and continuous love.

Yoga Tchouzar is not the source of Sengueï Ngaro; it is only a skillful means, and bodhicitta is the source. This bodhicitta is at the heart of Yoga Tchouzar. Within the emblem of Sengueï Ngaro, it is represented by the "tall cascade of bodhicitta," which extinguishes the flames of anger.

The Tibetan expression *tchouzar* refers mainly to the element water, but in its yoga context the practice includes all four elements:* earth, water, fire, and air. These four elements are considered in Sengueï Ngaro as being principles of solidity and stability, wetness and fluidity, heat and luminosity, and mobility and lightness.

THE LAMA WARRIOR'S ATTIRE

Since the beginning of Sengueï Ngaro, the particular attire of the lama warriors has always used the colors saffron, red, and black. The art of Sengueï Ngaro comes from the region of Kham in Tibet, and this clothing was worn only by the lama warriors, called khampas, who worked with Sengueï Ngaro. Their martial art, which was practiced in secret in a monastery, required a clothing design that combined the loose fit necessary for the practice of a martial art with respect for monastic discipline.

This kind of clothing—a long saffron tunic cinched with a wide red belt, over a long-sleeved shirt and black pants—is related to dharma vinaya. The dharma, or doctrine, set forth in discourses (sutras) but also

---

*These four elements are called in Tibetan *byung ba bzhi.*

in later texts (*tantras*) is represented respectively by the saffron-colored tunic and its red-colored belt. This clothing also represents *vinaya*, or discipline, the rules of training and obedience that regulate the daily life of monks.

This tunic is worn only by those fully inducted into Sengueï Ngaro, the lama warriors who have received all of the martial arts techniques. The other practitioners usually wear only black.

In the art of Sengueï Ngaro, each color has a meaning. In fact, black-colored clothing allows the practitioner's light to radiate outward and also prevents negativity from penetrating inside. This is the spiritual armor of the lama warrior. From black, all colors can arise. There's nothing negative about black. It represents the world of the *dharmapalas,* the "protectors of the dharma," and is the color of protection.

The color black has been used in the design of the hats of the karmapas, and is also featured on the hats of the Tcham dancers of Tibet. There is also a tradition of Tibetan painting called *nag thank.**

Many traditional martial artists, regardless of their cultural origin, wear black attire, but they very often forget its deep meaning. Primarily, it means that we can help others who are in danger without putting ourselves in danger. It's not about being able to hit without being hit or training to become a dark side warrior. Rather, it's about being able to radiate light, like the lotus, without being sullied by negativity. The lotus is rooted in the earth. It grows up from the dirt, spreading its budding blossom into the air above, then turns toward the fire of the sun, and finally opens out into space.

Just as the lotus springs forth from the mud and radiates the beauty and purity of its immaculate flower into the light, if we are to serve others, so, too, must our gift of protection be accomplished first and foremost through radiating the light of wisdom.

---

* Abbreviation of *nagpo thangka,* black thangka, or black painting. The greater part of the background in this style of painting is the color black, combined with dark blue, red, green, or yellow.

SENGUEÏ NGARO AND MEDITATION

☯ *Meditation*

The excellent techniques of Sengueï Ngaro include practices associated with meditation, contemplation, and yoga. (See plate 1.) Since these teachings are kept secret and are transmitted only individually, it would be almost impossible to describe them all, or to delineate their essential points to make them understandable and beneficial to everyone.

One day, Lama Tra made the following suggestion to me: "Because every person is different and has his own capabilities and difficulties specific to his individual progress, Sengueï Ngaro has several skillful means available. It is important to use them wisely, at a precise moment, at a precise place, and for a particular practitioner. This is why numerous meditation practices are kept secret. If a particular skillful means or remedy is used at the wrong moment, in the wrong amount, in the wrong place, or is not adapted to the right person, then such a remedy will turn into poison, and is more likely to do harm to the suffering person than to promote his healing."

There are many kinds of meditation in Sengueï Ngaro. Meditation itself could be described and examined in a number of books or, as in the Dzogchen tradition, spelled out in just a few words. But in any case, what is very important for anyone wanting to learn to meditate is first of all to find a qualified teacher, so that one can receive individual guidance.

Nevertheless, I'm going to explain how to bring your mind into contemplation and how to find calm and the natural state in yourself. You just need to sit down with the torso upright. It doesn't matter if you sit in the lotus position, or the half lotus, on a chair, on a rock, or in an armchair.

Diving into meditation doesn't mean taking a siesta or relaxing by letting your mind wander all over the place. Nor is it imagining things or dreaming about splendiferous results. It's also not about wanting to reach something transcendental. Unlike all that, meditation is to be found in immanence and in letting go. What's required above all is to lead your mind into freeing itself from what the Buddha called "the five hindrances."

1. *Clear away worldly longing by freeing your thoughts of all desire.* In order to purify this desire, it is important right away to expect nothing from the meditation, not to look for anything. Wanting to meditate is a good thing, but meditating while wanting is something else. When you sit down to meditate, it is good to develop correct motivation and correct devotion to your teacher right away.

    To practice Sengueï Ngaro is primarily to put all beings before yourself. Training yourself to do this, and not putting yourself above others, will allow you to have the right attitude for uprooting desire. From that moment on, you can begin to really enter into the state of meditation.

2. *Uproot anger by developing an authentic compassion for all sentient beings.* To purify this anger, you must begin by being more concerned about the welfare of others than about your own comfort on your meditation cushion.

    His Holiness the Dalai Lama made a commentary on the wishes that are traditionally recited during meditative practices, in which it is said, "May we help beings!" He made it clear that it would be better to say, "May I help beings!" and that perhaps by saying from the bottom of your heart "Starting right now I'm going to help beings!" you would be a little more engaged. Or even by stating sincerely, "Today I helped beings and tomorrow I'll do my best to help them again." That's the best attitude, real compassion: the authentic action of a bodhisattva.

    This is also the underlying message of Sengueï Ngaro. It's not about expressing a wish and developing compassion with words; you have to practice and cultivate it relentlessly, on every occasion that arises, through your thoughts, words, and then actions—and especially during meditation or when you find yourself faced by a situation of conflict.

3. ***Reject lethargy and indolence by striving to keep the mind free of laziness.***

You can see many meditators seated in a temple, motionless and unshakable as mountains. Very often they're falling asleep and are not getting any benefit from their meditation session. If you are meditating in order to sink comfortably into a lazy attitude, it would be better to have a nap or even to go to work; it would perhaps be more useful and more profitable. For some it would perhaps be better to do some stretching exercises, yoga, or dance than to do Sengueï Ngaro, because the art of Sengueï Ngaaro is not just gymnastics, a pastime, or the art of relaxing.

In order to distance oneself from this indolence, which is often very subtle, the practitioner of Sengueï Ngaro must develop clarity of mind and attention, but also self-mastery. For that, your best friend will be discriminating watchfulness, which will help you combat dullness and agitation when they threaten to disrupt your state of meditative balance.

In an aggressive situation, if you meet your aggressor's attack by remaining lethargic or by rushing into a counterattack, it could be fatal. Likewise, if you remain vigilant when faced with the multiple assaults of several aggressors and drop your attention before the last aggressor has been dealt with, that, too, will be fatal.

4. ***Eradicate distraction and agitation while remaining calm and peaceful inside.*** In order to purify your mental state and inner agitation, it is beneficial to observe yourself. The movement of your body and your breathing will very often reveal your distractions, which are sometimes coarse and other times quite subtle.

The art of Sengueï Ngaro teaches us that sitting still is not all it takes to meditate. Let's take an example: If you move a glass full of water across the table, the water will be agitated a little, and the more quickly you move it, the more agitated the water will be. Sometimes a single movement is enough to spill the whole thing. What is fundamental to the practice of meditation is to move the glass without agitating the water. Self-mastery, then, is to be found in the reality of not losing a single drop.

Sitting motionless, in silence, in a state of imperturbable meditation may seem easy to attain, even if it takes years of long training. However, setting your body and breathing into movement to counter an aggressor's attack and simultaneously maintaining calm and concentration on a point, is a much more difficult practice to master. This is why my teacher, Lama Tra, often said to me, "Settling down your body and quieting your breathing are one thing, but focusing your mind on one point is something else again."

In fact, meditating while the mind stays preoccupied with what you saw beforehand, or by what you're going to be eating soon, will not lead you into a state of concentration or deepen your practice of meditation. In the same way, if your legs hurt and you can't stop thinking of when you're going to be able to relax the body's posture, then the mind will stay attached to this suffering, which will spread from the legs to the whole being. The meditation will end up becoming unbearable. In such cases, it's good to relax the legs for a few moments before picking up the meditation again. You can even get up and go see what's cooking in the kitchen! Meditation is not to be found in simply not moving and turning into frozen meat.

5. *Get rid of doubt by removing uncertainty about good thoughts, good words, and even good actions.*

In order to purify this doubt, you need to allow your mind to remain in its natural state without conceptual elaboration, and without constantly thinking up fixes. Sengueï Ngaro teaches that the first thought is always the right one. You must not doubt when you're faced with an aggressor. Doubt leads to mistakes

15. *Form of the eighty-six movements: guard.*

16. Posture of Dordjé Drolö

17. Form of the eighty-six movements: guard.

18. *Form of the forty-two palms of the Buddha: picking the flower.*

19. *Form of the forty-two palms of the Buddha.*

20. Form of the eight short movements and the eight long movements: long lateral stride.

21. Form of the ten animals: the mongoose.

22. Form of the ten animals: the crane.

23. Form of the ten animals: the crane.

24. *Form of the wind horse: the snow lion.*

25. *Form of the wind horse: the tiger.*

26. Form of the ten circles.

and weakens motivation. If you maintain the attitude of the bodhisattva, then such an attitude can never be sullied by doubt, whether it's before, during, or after a situation of aggression.

For example, it's common to change the direction in which you look every three seconds and your body posture every five minutes. Of course, these movements of the body and changes in visual direction correspond to energy circulation, as you gradually penetrate into the depths of your natural state. But the important thing is not to doubt! Certain training that is unique to Sengueï Ngaro is done blindfolded, eradicating this doubt that invades at every moment. This kind of training is actually a real meditation practice.

These are extremely valuable instructions left by the masters of Sengueï Ngaro. Every person, even if he is not a lama warrior, who wants to meditate with sincerity and motivation must be inspired by these instructions so he can abandon the five hindrances. And such a person, having rid himself of them, will then be able to really engage in self-contemplation.

The Buddha himself said:

> *As one finds a way out of debt,*
> *Out of illness, out of prison, out of slavery,*
> *Out of a path in the desert,*
> *Thus a monk finds a way out of these five hindrances*
> *And engages in contemplation of the self.*

THE GLASS OF WATER EXERCISE

Practicing meditation doesn't necessarily require numerous instructions from your teacher. For example, all you need to do is to sit down and stare at a point in front of you. Gradually, the body, the breathing, and

---

*Cimentapada.

thoughts will naturally become calm and you will be released from the five hindrances.

I'm going to tell you a story. It's about a five-year-old boy named Gabriel. He was always very agitated both when he was awake and when he was asleep. He was overflowing with energy, as in the previously mentioned example of the glass full of water being moved across the table. It actually was rare in his case for there to be any water left in the bottom of the glass!

At first glance, it seemed almost impossible for this boy to meditate without fidgeting, getting upset in all kinds of ways, babbling, or plunging into his imaginary world where his mind loved to wander. Many of those close to him were stunned to learn that Gabriel succeeded in remaining still, seated in meditation, opposite a simple glass full of water, and that he continued that way for more than an hour without interruption.

How did this young boy succeed?

The exercise consisted in contemplating the surface of the water and realizing that, if you didn't move the glass, the water would not be agitated. So, too, if you didn't agitate the body and the breathing, the mind would remain unagitated and at rest. In order to coordinate all the energies of the body, the breathing, and the mind, the exercise consisted of keeping a little golden pinecone balanced on the top of the head. You had to keep it there as long as possible without it falling off, while the mind remained fixed on the glass of water.

Once the exercise was finished, little Gabriel began to practice it on his own as a game, doing his best to remain still as long as he had the first time. After that his behavior was vastly different; he became much less agitated and disturbed in his sleep.

Besides this, he developed certain qualities specific to meditation, and sometimes announced unforeseeable events to his mother. His clarity of mind was a surprise for someone of his young age. Being surprised himself by this kind of foresight, he developed a taste for meditation and still continues to practice, even without the pinecone.

I recommend this exercise to agitated people regardless of their age. There is nothing simpler. Just sit down and look at your glass of water. You can even do it at work! Everyone who says he's stressed out can test the effectiveness of this kind of meditation. It may be that some will no longer need to take an antidepressant to calm down; just keeping a glass of water on the table might be sufficient.

CHAPTER NINE

THE FOUR ELEMENTS

WATER

◈ *The Great Waterfall of Bodhicitta*

On the emblem of Sengueï Ngaro, there is the image of a great waterfall springing forth from a gigantic mountain. It's called the great cascade of bodhicitta: great because its bountiful spray touches all beings of the six classes and ripens the fruit of Awakening; and bodhicitta because, like mercury, it whitens all the blemishes of karma and the emotions.

The great cascade of bodhicitta has the velvety sheen of the conch, the color of freshly fallen snow, and the clarity of the full moon. Its waters are endowed with the eight qualities.* In the emblem of Yoga Tchouzar, the waterfall is represented as putting out flames. The waters of this great cascade, clothed in white silk, are reputed to lessen the suffering of beings by spreading gentleness and coolness. Its harmonious voice goes straight to the heart and puts out the flames of anger. This anger, so difficult to control and calm, will little by little, because of the continuous flow of bodhicitta, be transmuted into love and compassion for all beings without exception.

---

*Coolness, excellent taste and smell, lightness, gentleness, clarity, luminosity, and benefits the throat and stomach if ingested.

☯ The Wisdom of Water

Water is the matrix of all conceivable forms in the universe; it models them and sets them vibrating. In the practice of Senguëi Ngaro, we have a profound teaching that is very important for the knowledge of nature and the essence of its elements.

Taoist wisdom has really inspired the practitioners of *Tai chi chuan.** And in the Tibetan tradition of Senguëi Ngaro, we also find this practice of observation and retreat into nature.

Nature is, in fact, the cradle of all forms; it is the primal mother of all traditional martial arts. Jiguro Kano was inspired to create the first judo techniques through observing the branches of a tree that bent without breaking, enabling heavy layers of snow to fall to the ground. Moreishi Ueshiba, the founder of Aikido, was said to execute his movements in harmony with the elements and with the earth's rotation. It's the same with many traditional martial arts.

In the Tibetan tradition of the Nyingma school there is, in fact, a retreat practice that consists of spending several days in nature in order to observe each element, one after the other. Then the student returns to his teacher to share his discoveries and what he has attained in his meditative practice.

Being able to unite with the elements—meditating under an icy waterfall in the middle of winter or walking on burning coals—requires first that you learn to observe and understand how the element manifests and acts. Each element is divided into multiple realities with a unique form, essence, quality, and proper function. Without that, the practice would bring no benefit other than to overcome fear a little, or to reinforce pride.

What, then, is the wisdom of water? The water of the cascade purifies, maintains, and regenerates. It inseminates and engenders the various forms of life on the planet. Its changing aspect, and the speed with

---

*This martial art also has gestures that combine the four elements. These gestures are called "the thirteen postures."

which water moves from one state to another, shows how it is both material and formless: an element that is able to make thousands of changes.

Through its flow and its perpetual renewal, it can take any outward form—a lake, a cloud, or a waterfall, as on the mandala of Yoga Tchouzar. Everywhere that water rises up, the countryside is transformed by this current of life that nourishes, destroys, and purifies. All destruction leads to regeneration.

By meditating on this element, experiences can arise and we can come to wisdom from the water. This is why, in Yoga Tchouzar, there are specific advanced meditation practices that take place in winter under high waterfalls.

Certain natural cascades that don't have any dams upstream and are oriented to the east, or which have various other precise criteria, are favored over others. But this involves teachings that are very secret and are revealed only to lama warriors who progress to these kinds of practices—practices that are called "excellent."

There is no merit or result to be obtained if you think that by meditating for several hours under a winter cascade you're definitely going to come to Awakening. You'd be just like a frog hunched over in the water. Frogs have been in water for a long time and haven't arrived at Awakening! In fact, there's a joke about this by the Buddha himself, aimed at the Brahmins who were practicing this kind of asceticism in India. Buddhist teaching is the middle way, and this is why Senguëi Ngaro does not recommend delving into extremes of asceticism.

These experiences are part of being a practitioner of Yoga Tchouzar, and part of one's evolution in meditative practice. If certain experiences arise, they are spontaneous and impossible to put into simple words. Some yogis have composed whole collections of "adamantine songs," called *dohas,* which are capable of describing some of these meditative experiences. The most famous ones are by the yogis Milarepa, Shabkar, and even the famous yogi Drukpa Kunley.

However, if you have never experienced this type of ascetic practice for yourself, or have never meditated on nature and the essence of the elements, then you won't find any benefit from this type of song. The words are only a shell, and the experience is the kernel that you must taste yourself in order to be able to appreciate what a delicious food it is.

"The Song of the Great Adamantine Cascade" explains one of these experiences, specific to Yoga Tchouzar. I composed it at the time of a meditative practice under a cascade named Druk Ksar.[1]

> *Kyema Ho!*
> *May the cascade of a thousand vajras,*
> *Shining with the white light that illuminates all,*
> *Bring to all beings the wisdom of the mirror*
> *In the rain of a thousand clear-eyed diamonds.*
>
> *May the cascade of a thousand* ratnas,*
> *Springing forth from a yellow light that harmonizes*
> *   all,*
> *Bring to all beings the wisdom of identity*
> *In the rain of a thousand multicolored jewels.*
>
> *May the cascade of a thousand* padmas,†
> *Enlightening with red light the whole of infinity,*
> *Bring to all beings the wisdom of clear, discriminating*
> *   vision*
> *In the rain of a thousand white lotuses.*
>
> *May the cascade of a thousand* khadgas,‡
> *Protectress of the green light that accomplishes all,*

---

*In Tibetan, *ratna* is the word for "jewel."
†In Tibetan, *padma* is the word for "lotus."
‡In Tibetan, *khadgas* is the word for "swords."

Bring to all beings the wisdom that realizes all
In the rain of a thousand flaming swords.

May the cascade of a thousand Buddhas,
Radiating with the blue light that unifies all,
Bring to all beings the wisdom of emptiness
In the rain of a thousand wheels of gold.

May the great cascade of bodhicitta,
Illuminating with the velvety brightness of the white
    conch,
Bring to all beings the wisdom of Dharmadhatu
In the rain of a thousand thigle* *rainbows.*

EARTH

☯ The Refuge Island

You might think that by going to meditate under waterfalls, the practitioner of Sengueï Ngaro is distancing himself from reality. In fact, the isolation of the lama warrior is neither a retreat nor hiding, nor is it a flight or a refuge in the midst of disaster. It means bringing yourself back to the island that you are, by strengthening yourself against the wind and the tides so that ultimately you can regain other worlds through the way of the waters: bodhicitta.

This is part of the symbolism of the "mountain-island" of Yoga Tchouzar that is represented on the emblem of Sengueï Ngaro. It is a kind of "refuge island." The basic symbolism of this impressive mountain originates in both Buddhist and Tibetan cosmology, where it is said that in the principle behind all things is a blessed land in the middle of the waters. This island, which is also a mountain, is the transcendent

---

*In Tibetan, *thigle* is a technical term in Dzogchen, which could be translated in this context as "subtle, vital energy."

link where earth joins heaven, and where the various kingdoms of deities are arrayed.*

This great mountain represents the highest point on earth, the point where we reach heaven. This is why this holy land bears the name Celestial Land (Svarga Bhoumi), Golden Land (Suvarna Bhoumi), or Land of Joy (Tushita Bhoumi), engendering both fear and wonderment simultaneously. For Tibetans, the mountain is sacred, the refuge of deities and yogis.

☯ Mount Meru

This mountain-island is, in a way, the fixed pole of the cosmos, as is seen in ancient shamanic traditions.

In Tibet, the Bön tradition had this representation of the universe:† the mountain as the dynamic center from which adamantine energy spreads out through the four directions of space across the phenomenal universe. For this reason, it is also called "middle island" (*madhya dvipas*); "island continent," from which Mount Meru rises up—meaning the mountain with a lake—and the "great islands" or "great continents" (*maha dvipas*)—four great regions seen as "island continents."

Bringing yourself back to the island means you are depending on only your own essential nature and the essential nature of phenomena: emptiness. Someone who doesn't realize the emptiness of self and of phenomena has little chance of progressing in the ascetic practices of Yoga Tchouzar, and will miss the essence of Sengueï Ngaro. "Strengthening the self against the wind and the tides" means overcoming obstacles, trials, and emotions through the realization of emptiness.

---

*The divinities are ranked and arranged based on degrees of exact spiritual elevation, sometimes being assigned to three major classes: the Lha (gods), men, and the subterraneous divinities (Klu). (See Chögyur Lingpa, *Tara sadhana:* Montignac, Ed. Padmakara, 1986.)

†Mount Kailash, the source of four great rivers, is the center of the universe for the Bönpo, as for the Hindus. This symbolism is retained in the Bön emblem *yung drung,* a swastika in which the four arms and the center represent the five elements.

The immovable mountain is the symbol of emptiness. Unless this is realized, the practice of Sengueï Ngaro is pointless and without success.

☯ The Obstacle Mountain

The concept of obstacle is also linked to the symbolism of this gigantic, insurmountable mountain. Being the site of specific phenomena, the mountain can, in fact, suit the image of a refuge mountain or an obstacle mountain. On the one hand, you find there conditions that are favorable for meditating, notably the presence of the five elements. On the other hand, very far from offering a route to its snowy, icy peaks, the mountain often blocks the path with ramparts, avalanches, torrents, storms, glaciers, and intense suffering.

It is for this reason that, in the tradition of Sengueï Ngaro,* as in Japan, the mountain is often associated with trials and forbidden ways. It is also the abode of the "four brothers who ride the summits": the tiger, the snow lioness, the garuda, and the dragon. The four animals mainly symbolize four elements (earth, water, fire, and air).

"Regaining other worlds through the way of the waters" means, then, through the continual flowing of the spirit of Awakening. Like the cascade, *sita,* one opens oneself to the world around one and is reborn equipped with the armor of the spirit of Awakening.

☯ The Inseminating Island

The mountain-island, a symbol of emptiness, would then be represented as something like a place of spiritual rebirthing. In Tibetan, the term *ling* has the following meanings: "island," "place," and "garden."†

The uterine reference of the island, which stems from its amniotic symbolism, represents it as a place of rebirth in which the Sengueï Ngaro apprentice becomes a warrior through the awareness of himself as

---

*This tradition has continued in the Shintoist and Buddhist traditions, such as in the Shingon and Tendai schools, as well as in the ascetic schools of Shugendo and the Yamabushi (mountain warriors).

†This term is found in many place-names, for example, Darjeeling: place of the dordjé.

a sacred island, an island reduced to its essential nature and surrounded by the fascinating other world of the open sea. Such a warrior will be able to consider incursions in the four directions of the universe, each of which will be characterized by an activity: pacification, growth, power, or destruction. He will then choose his own direction, beginning the spiritual adventure of the warrior armed with the spirit of Awakening.

This philosophy of Sengueï Ngaro is very close to the path of the warrior of Awakening revealed by Chogyam Trungpa.[2] He put it this way: "The challenge of warriorship is to step out of the cocoon, to step out into space, by being brave and at the same time gentle."

That's how a lion would behave.

The mountain-island, then, has a double symbolic aspect: fertilizing the mind so that it realizes emptiness and rebirthing the mind so that it becomes compassionate. Insofar as it is a mountain, it ensures the propagating function. It engenders streams, precious stones, plants, fabled trees, beneficent springs, and waterfalls; but also air and clouds containing rain, snow, and hail; as well as the fire of volcanoes and lightning. And then, insofar as it is an island, it is reminiscent of the mystery of gestation, the fetal life that surrounds itself with water from the beginning; and the rebirth into a new universe, stripped of all impurity and aggression.

AIR

In the emblem of Sengueï Ngaro there is a cloud moving toward the north. It's hooked on the peak of the mountain. This is its symbolism: like the five *skandhas,* the clouds drift here and there and, at a certain moment, dissipate and disappear. As long as the cloud of unknowing covers the sky, bringing a double darkness, nothing can be distinguished clearly. Chasing the cloud of the two veils—the double obscurity that covers the blue of the sky and the light of the sun—the yogi causes the wind to blow, refreshing the six pathways so that the cloud of the law appears, and so that beneficent snow falls abundantly on the three burning environments. Once the tenth land is reached, you will receive the annointing of the bodhisattvas through great knowledge.

◎ *The Cloud of Impermanence*

The cloud of the five skandhas symbolizes the impermanence of the elements. It is the very symbol of the visible metamorphosis of water in its becoming: the ascension of earthly water into celestial water—mainly through the action of the elements of fire and air—which then falls back down from the sky in various forms. Because the cloud harbors both the storm and beneficent rain, it contains also the forces of snow, hail, and lightning. The cloud is there to remind you of the impermanence of the beings in this universe. As it is stressed in *L'Immense Déploiement* (The Vast Array):

> *The beings of the three worlds are as ephemeral as the*
> *clouds in the sky.*

By meditating on impermanence—first on that of the universe, using the image of the cloud that melts away, destroyed by the wind, then on the impermanence of the beings inhabiting the universe—you will develop the conviction that death is inevitable. Each heartbeat reduces your life span a little more and brings you a little closer to death. Even though you don't know the hour of your death, it comes inexorably closer, like the cascade that rushes down the mountainside.

Meditation on death releases you from attachment and hatred, and can help you realize the equality of all things. It can also invigorate your practice and maintain courage in your practice of giving protection.

At the level of the mind, the cloud of unknowing (*marigpa* in Tibetan) symbolizes the fundamental ignorance that is at the root of emotions and which entails a double obfuscation: that created by the passions and that created by knowledge.

If you desire omniscience and liberation from the cloud of unknowing, you must cultivate meditation on emptiness, because this is how the double obfuscation can be destroyed, making way for the wisdom of rigpa to come. It is through profound meditation on emptiness that all phenomena and all existences will be revealed in their relative nature and melt away. At just that moment, the power of the mind is such that the perception of all phenomena does not destroy the meditation on emptiness, because the subtle veils that obscure the mind have been eliminated.

The cloud of the two veils covering the blue sky and the radiating light of the sun can be compared to the thick clouds that blanket the hilltops with fog and the valleys with shadows, or to the rain clouds that shroud the mountain peaks. When the cloud of the two veils is driven away, wisdom appears, clear and immaculate as the sun.

☯ The Cloud of the Law

The cloud of the dharma is also known as the cloud of great knowledge of the law, since it carries the water of merit and allows beings to develop.

The cloud is called "of the dharma," since just as all clouds that are charged with nourishing rain will bring forth harvests, the bodhisattva, through the agency of the dharma, will be able to bring the virtuous actions of all beings to fruition.

To do that, the bodhisattva suppresses the imprint of the *kleshas,* the veils, and the number of his powers then becomes infinite. In order to suppress this subtle imprint, he must drive away the cloud of the two veils with the wind of bodhicitta.

The wind that freshens the six roads is very closely connected with the fact that the cloud is itself associated with the element of air. The wind that freshens the six roads symbolizes the wind of bodhicitta that the practitioner of Sengueï Ngaro develops for the six classes of beings. The six stages through which beings must pass are as follows:

- The road of hell-beings
- The road of hungry ghosts

- The road of animals
- The road of humans
- The road of demigods
- The road of the gods

Through this action of the spirit of Awakening, the practitioner of Sengueï Ngaro must develop a great compassion for the beings of the three places of fire: first, hell; then, the place of blood—the animals that devour each other; and finally, the burning place of weapons—men who make war.

Why these three places in particular? Because all three are connected with anger and aggression. In the place of fire, for example, there are several levels, according to Buddhist tradition. One of these, Samjiva, concerns guilty beings who, over thousands of years, are killed and killed again,* embarking on life each time only to be killed again. Their karma is such that they always see the people they encounter as enemies, and they cut open each other's chests with their long, sharp nails that are pointed like daggers. According to Buddhist texts, those who lead men into war, or those who take pleasure in the art of combat, will be born again in this kingdom in order to expiate their acts.

I'm telling you this since it's a very important teaching for those who devote themselves to the world of weapons and who take pleasure in fighting, competition, combat, and hunting.

In fact, there are martial arts where you can stray very far from the principal aim: the spirit of Awakening. Sengueï Ngaro is an art for preserving life, not an art for ending it. You must strive to obtain self-mastery and not seek power over others. Buddhist wisdom—which

---

*The first of these hells is named Yan sos, because the beings there kill each other in unending combat. Voices, which are created by their own actions, call them back to life to battle once again.

has numerous teachings on this subject, including the laws of karma, the different worlds of existence, the sufferings in hell, and so on— teaches the absolute necessity of cultivating the spirit of Awakening before all else.

Meditating on each of these three levels of existence is a practice that every martial art should include, because it really demonstrates something about human nature, a nature that is often closer to hell-beings, or animals that devour each other, than to any kind of humanity. In these three places, the beings do not know bodhicitta, the spirit of Awakening.

The place of blood resembles all the animals that suffer and struggle for survival. Take time to observe this unending combat between species. The larger eat the smaller and the smallest nibble away at the biggest. Some live in constant fear and concern that they will be devoured by fiercer beings or killed by hunters.

Such meditation brings real meaning to the practice of an authentic martial art and can give rise to, maintain, and foster boundless compassion for all beings without exception.

⊙ The Anointing of the Bodhisattvas

The practitioner who attains the tenth land receives the anointing of the bodhisattvas through great knowledge. It is a blessing, even in our times, to have very great masters who have attained this level of spiritual realization. They are quite rare and precious. I am not qualified enough to speak of this, but I'm going to try to explain as best I can. The tenth land belongs to the lands called *bhoumi,* "lands of knowledge," where every act is actualized through knowledge. During the anointing of the bodhisattvas in the tenth land, the Buddhas moisten the top of the heads of these bodhisattvas with the water of knowledge: this is called "the anointing of the bodhisattvas through great knowledge."

This anointing may also take the form of a beneficent rain. In the Mahayana teachings we often find the image of the body of the Buddha floating like a cloud above the mountain and moving to the north. He pours out the rain of the beneficent law for all beings. This rain reaches even the smallest parcel of land, and falls into the limitless vase beneath.

The great knowledge means, then, that the knowledge of all the boddhisatvas conforms to the reality of the ten subtle categories of knowledge of the Buddhas.

These categories are named as follows:

Knowledge of practice,
Knowledge of birth and death,
Knowledge of the world,
Knowledge of the way out of the family,
Knowledge of complete, manifest Awakening,
Knowledge of the mastery of spiritual force,
Knowledge of the act of turning the wheel of the law,
Knowledge of power over the duration of life,
Knowledge of the manifestation of nirvana,
Knowledge of permanent support of the law.

FIRE

☯ *Meri Barwa: The Fire Peak*

On the mandala of Yoga Tchouzar, a part of the mountain is in flames. This is the "fire peak," called Meri Barwa in Tibetan—the flaming mountain. This refers to a mythical place, situated to the north, where a myriad host of protectors of Sengueï Ngaro assemble. It's a bit like a volcano or a furnace. This living fire springs up from the flaming peak and devours the freshly fallen snow.

This is a great mountain with slopes on one side coated in ice and on the other slopes ablaze with fire. This mountain corresponds to the fire element in the ascetic practices of Yoga Tchouzar.

☉ *The Wisdom of Fire*

What does this wisdom of fire represent? The presence of the fire of bodhicitta symbolizes that the mind has come to renunciation in the right way: renunciation of a cherishing of oneself in favor of developing a right motivation that benefits all beings.

This kind of fiery peak can be seen in certain Tibetan paintings depicting various Tibetan wrathful deities, or sometimes *mahasiddhas*, realized yogis, like Khadgapa, who holds a flaming sword. Certain mandalas, which depict eight cemeteries around their perimeters, also contain various traditional symbols, notably eight blazing fires. In this particular case, the cemeteries symbolize renunciation and the fires symbolize emptiness.

This is the fire of wisdom because this fire, which spreads out into space, is the symbol of the wisdom that is needed in order to set out on the spiritual path and to understand the meaning of the dharma. This living knowledge has four attributes: it is said to be profound, clear, extensive, and quick. The fire of wisdom can be compared to a tempest raging in all quarters. The rays of light that emanate from this fiery peak, differing in size and coming from different directions, bring benefit to all beings who are in the darkness of ignorance. Certain Tibetan deities, such as Dordjé Neljorma,* emanate this red fiery light from their bodies, thereby symbolizing that the state of happiness/emptiness emits a light that chases darkness from the mind.

In the practice of Yoga Tchouzar there are several meanings for this fiery peak. Seven terrifying flames spring up from its heart. They are like the apocalyptic fire spreading out to region upon region. During the day, the devouring flames of the seven qualities shoot out from the burning mountain. Like the tongues of serpents, they erase anything that has taken refuge in the musty reaches of duality. During the night, the wind of karma hurls the fire of wisdom in all directions, roaring like

---

*Vajra Yogini is usually represented surrounded by an immense fiery blaze, since she intensively practices *tummo* and burns with the fire of empty felicity.

a tempest and consuming in an instant the whole range of inner adversities as well as negative external forces. Since it seeks neither to flee nor to oppose with resistance, the mind of the practitioner of Sengueï Ngaro, indistinguishable from the fire of the wrathful ones, then melts into the clear light that is unified with emptiness.

☯ The Seven Flames

Seven terrible flames spring up from the fiery peak. When Sengueï Ngaro speaks of the qualities of fire, it is based on precise observation of the qualities inherent in this element, which the masters of the past learned to observe, meditate upon, and perform skillfully. All this comes originally from an ancient Vedic tradition in India, where the ritual of fire had been practiced for thousands of years. This tradition moved into Tibet, where numerous fire rituals were maintained and practiced. Some consisted of offerings of consecrated substances to the fire,* while others, as in the techniques of Sengueï Ngaro, referred to yoga practices that aim to master this element.

In meditating on the element of fire, it is important to distinguish between the two principal natures of fire: one is the heat and devouring energy of the flame and the other is its clarity and beneficent light. Building on that, there are seven inherent qualities in the flame. In ancient India, these seven qualities were personified as seven wrathful goddesses.†

If you begin to observe a wood fire, you will be able to contemplate these distinct kinds of flames, and the seven qualities of fire, like seven

---

*In this connection, there are Tibetan rituals such as Riwo sang chö, Sur chö, Jintsek, and so on.

†Here are the seven: The three goddesses who are compared to the three flames of the lower worlds are "the dark one," "the terrifying and gaping one with the dreadful teeth," and "the one who has the quality of being as quick as lightning or thought." Those corresponding to the flames of the upper worlds are "the one who is blood red," "the one who is very dark red and veiled in smoke," and "the one who gives off sparks." The seventh is called "she who has within her all the brilliance, all the colors, and all the beauty."

goddesses, will perhaps appear as you contemplate the deep nature of the fire.

In fact, the fiery peak burns even more intensely than these seven kinds of flame. This is why it is compared to the end-time fire, the terrible fire that bursts forth at the end of a cosmic cycle, or *kalpa.* It is said to be so intense that it spreads out to region upon region destroying all adversities, all mental veils, all diseases, and all habitual tendencies; as well as all negative external forces, such as harmful and aggressive beings, powerful evil forces, and negative spirits that give rise to epidemics, wars, and other scourges.

◎ *The Seven Qualities of the Fire of Tummo*

The seven qualities of the fire of wisdom correspond to the qualities of the inner fire, called tummo, or psychic heat, in Tibetan yoga It is this psychic heat that must be developed by the Tibetan yogis during their ascetic practices in the elements, particularly during their lives as wandering hermits in the solitude of the high mountains of Tibet.

The practice of tummo, which is an element of Yoga Tchouzar, comes out of this tradition. It is also used when carrying out certain martial arts forms that are specific to the art of the lama warriors of Sengueï Ngaro, notably in the practice of the form of the forty-two palms of the Buddha. (See pages 105–7 in chapter 5.)

The flames of wisdom are said to have seven qualities: they are burning, virulent, violent, penetrating, powerful, strong, and quick. The breathing practice of tummo leads to a complete transformation of energies on the spiritual as well as physical level. We speak, then, of the tummo of the body and of its sublimation into tummo of the mind. This breathing not only raises or lowers the body heat, but also leads to a real transformation of the mind by consuming all veils, obstacles, concepts, and so on.

A spontaneous song on the deep meaning of this psychic heat was given to me by the Venerable Khatok Rigdzin Tchenpo, the last one to sit in the Khatok throne. It was composed by this great yogi in homage to the lama warriors of Sengueï Ngaro. This song describes the essence of tummo. Here is part of it:

> *Through*
> *The heat and ecstasy that has flamed out in the body*
> *And the tummo of the ultimate meaning that has been*
> *   realized in the mind*
> *May you vanquish with the fire of primordial wisdom*
> *All the emotions embedded in the breath and in the mind*
> *All veils, all concepts . . .*

However, in order to produce the heat of bliss from tummo, it takes more than being able to meditate in the icy water of a river or a cascade, or to dress only in simple cotton clothing in the middle of winter, as the yogis do. The great yogi Drukpa Kunley himself, in speaking about the ascetic practices that lead to the heat of bliss, exclaimed, "What will become of the one who right away wants to taste the cold hell of dressing in cotton if he doesn't know how to produce the heat of ecstasy?"

Developing this heat of ecstasy requires specific training and sustained instruction from a teacher. Without that, it is very easy to become quite lost or even to lose one's life. This is why these practices of Sengueï Ngaro are transmitted only after a complete apprenticeship in the profound and secret forms, since the physical and psychic energy of the student is then reinforced and sublimated.

PART FIVE

The Kingdom of Shambhala

CHAPTER TEN

SENGUEÏ NGARO
AND SHAMBHALA

THE EIGHT PROVINCES

One can view the central representation of Yoga Tchouzar as a blessed region or "pure ground," but it also can be considered the kingdom of Shambhala, the legendary location that gave birth to the art of Sengueï Ngaro. A *togden,* a realized hermit yogi living in a cave near the monastery of Lama Daidot, would transmit the secret principles of this martial art that he had received directly from the teachers of Shambhala. Thus the eight-spoked wheel in the emblem of Sengueï Ngaro describes the mythical land of Shambhala, a land divided into eight provinces. This fabled country is said to be protected by eight fortifications in the form of insurmountable mountains of ice.

It is said that each of the four underground mandalas is divided in half, creating eight regions. On the mandala of Yoga Tchouzar it's the same: there is the representation of the four elements, which are written in Tibetan and are divided in two, thus forming a second square. The composite then forms a wheel of eight points. At the center of this eight-petaled lotus is the fabled land of Shambhala.

The symbol of eight has always been kept in the martial arts base of Sengueï Ngaro. All the profound techniques, for example, are grouped by eight: the eight short fists, the eight long fists, the eight movement forms, the eight cycles of breathing, and so on.

THE FIVE ELEMENTS

The mountain that is drawn on the emblem of Yoga Tchouzar represents in some way the center of this country. The Kalachakra texts also speak of a mountain of molten iron, named the mountain of Vajra. According to the Kalachakra tantras from the Buddha, who describes this country, it is specified that the physical appearance, the dimensions, and the description of this kingdom of Shambhala vary according to the collective karma of sentient beings.

It is especially subtle to produce a detailed description and a precise location for the kingdom of Shambhala in the present day. The tantras describe it as the potentialities of the atoms of the five elements at the center of empty and unrestricted space.

Here there is a point in common between the emblem of Yoga Tchouzar and the five elements represented there, since it is said that the potentials of these five elements ensure the cohesion of the group of mandalas of the respective elements: earth, fire, water, and air.

KALACHAKRA AND SHAMBHALA

There is a historical connection between Shambhala and the teaching of the Buddha. At Dhanyakataka, in southern India, at the stupa of Amaravati, the Buddha conferred the initiation into the great mandala of Vajradhatu, as well as the tantra of the deity Kalachakra, in the presence of the king of Shambhala, named Suchandra, the Lord of the Perfect Moon, and an infinite number of gods, nagas, and humans.

It is said that the king scribed these ultimate teachings and that upon his return to his kingdom, he had a three-dimensional mandala of Kalachakra constructed. He also composed twelve hundred commentaries on this fundamental tantra, which is considered one of the nondual tantras. You can contemplate this mandala, produced in sand, during the Kalachakra initiations that His Holiness the Dalai Lama amazingly gives throughout the world. These very advanced initiations have the intention of bringing favorable circumstances for the establishment of universal peace.

The great masters from Shambhala propagated this doctrine in India and then into Tibet, where it was known and practiced.* The tradition has endured to the present day.

There are numerous Buddhist texts that describe this kind of pure kingdom. During my meeting with Geshe Ngawang Tashi in Dharamsala, he conveyed a part of the teaching that had been given by one of the principal tutors of His Holiness the Fourteenth Dalai Lama, His Holiness Kyabje Yongdzin Trijang Rinpoche.

This precious teaching of His Holiness Trijang Rinpoche is a brief response to certain questions asked of him about the kingdom of Shambhala. He then cites several texts, sutras, and *shastras* that describe this pure domain. Thinking that this text might be useful to all those who wish to deepen their knowledge of the country of Shambhala, Geshe Ngawang Tashi, on the day before my departure from Dharamsala, entrusted me with a copy of this teaching.†

---

*It is through three principal traditions that this teaching of the Kalachakra was introduced into Tibet: *dro, tsari,* and *ra.*

Kyabje Yongdzin Trijang Rinpoche was the second tutor of His Holiness Tenzin Gyatso, the Fourteenth Dalai Lama. This is why he carries the honorific title of *yongdzin,* which means "tutor." He was chosen by the Tibetan government for his advanced level of spiritual realization and for his extensive knowledge. This previous master left his body November 9, 1961. Since then, his reincarnation has been officially found and recognized.

†Geshe Ngawang Tashi is one of the senior officials of the famous monastery of Ganden, founded by Je Tsongkhapa and home since 1409 to newly graduated *kadampas,* also called *gelugpas.* Geshe Ngawang Tashi took great care in recopying in his own hand this teaching dating from 1965, which he kept carefully among his personal papers.

Here is what this text reveals about the secret kingdom of Shambhala:

> Where is the paradise of Shambhala to be found in the world? Is it
>   in the East or the West?
> Will Westerners be able to find it with their technology?
> Is it similar to a pure paradise that is devoid of suffering?
> Or instead does it have characteristics of a location that is part of
>   samsara?*

Here is what the great scholar Pelden Yeshe says on the subject of Shambhala:

> In the guiding texts, on the topic of going to Shambhala, it is
> said that it is a place found on this earth. Humans can go there
> on foot. It's a destination that we can reach by traveling steadily,
> helped by the magic power of mandalas of knowledge that let us
> travel into dangerous territory. These are certain mandalas of gods
> or genies.
>   There are also tales of travels to Shambhala in which Shambhala
> is compared to an impure field.†

In the present day it continues to be difficult to pinpoint the location of Shambhala on the terrestrial globe.

It's the same situation with the "glorious mountain of copper, light of the lotus," which is the country of the *rashasas*‡ in the southwest.

Shambhala, along with the structure of the universe with Mount Meru and the four continents, is described in the Avatamsaka sutra (Tibetan: *Do phal po che*).

---

*Questions asked in France by Gueche Loung-Rik Namgyal from the Gaden Chartse Monastery of His Holiness Yongzin Thridjang, veritable Vajradhara.
†An ordinary place.
‡Demons and ogres.

The paradises that exist in the celestial spheres, such as Dri me ö (Sphere of Immaculate Light), are described in "The Ocean of Pure Fields."

Those, which actually exist, are described in "The Ocean of Jewels, Luminous Essence of Appearances." Other explanations are given in numerous sutras and shastras (commentaries), such as:

"The Compendium of the Abhidharma" (*Ngönpa kuntu*)
"The Treasury of the Abhidharma" (*Ngönpa dzö*)
"The Pure Land Sutra" (*Djikten dakpa*)
"The Sutra of the Fixation of Attention" (*Drenpa nyer sha*)
"The Tantra of the Ocean of Dakinis" (*Gyu khandro gyatso*)
"The Kalachakra Tantra" (*Dus-kyi khorlo*).

THE KINGDOM OF SHAMBHALA

Externally, the kingdom of Shambhala is a circular configuration since it is surrounded by a chain of snowy mountains. Internally, it has the form of an eight-petaled lotus, each petal being separated by a broad flowing river. At its very heart, as in the bosom of a great blooming flower, is a gigantic mountain that dominates all with its brilliance. At the center of this vast country, under the gaze of four terrestrial continents, shimmers a beautiful city and a garden bearing the name Malaya. There are great lakes filled with jewels: to the east is Near Lake and to the west stretch the two White Lotus Lakes. The Palace, which has nine stories and is richly decorated with precious stones, is described in great detail in certain Buddhist texts.

That is a general description of the kingdom of Shambhala. This traditional description has already been set out by certain great Tibetan lamas, such as His Holiness the Fourteenth Dalai Lama and His Holiness Kalu Rinpoche, in order to shed more light on the link that connects the Kalachakra initiation and the kingdom of Shambhala.

Certain great realized masters, Tibetan *mahasiddhas** such as Orgyenpa and Jetsun Taranatha, have been to Shambhala and have written real travel guides describing the road that leads to this fantastic kingdom. One of the most famous guides is that of the Panchen Lama.

In addition, certain great teachers, through their pure vision or in a dream, have been able to transmit very precise descriptions and images of this invisible kingdom. Such is the case, for example, of a detailed vision given by the very Venerable Khamtrul Rinpoche. This lama had the opportunity to visit Shambhala in a dream, and has retained a very precise vision of it.[†]

As Geshe Ngawang Tashi has explained, there are also some esoteric texts that reveal particular aspects of this hidden kingdom. These texts were composed by hermit yogis who meditated in caves very close to the sacred territory of Shambhala. With their pure vision, these yogis, who in Tibetan are called *melong guru* (mirror teachers), were able to describe certain hidden aspects of this kingdom of Shambhala with great precision.

In this country called in Tibetan "the spring of happiness," the beings do not know of any distinction between "mine" and "yours," and they are unaware of the accumulation of earthly goods, so there is no jealousy or competition. The words *illness, war,* and *famine* do not exist. The happiness of these beings is said to be equal to that of the gods, and a deep and perfect peace reigns there. It is said that the inhabitants of that kingdom prosper based on their natural inner light.

So there is a real link between Shambhala and the art of Sengueï Ngaro. The oral tradition of Sengueï Ngaro makes clear that this martial art originates in Shambhala. Besides this detail, which comes from legend, it is essential to understand that Shambhala is associated with a

---

*Yogis with supernatural powers.
†Public teaching given by Khamtrul Rinpoche in New York in 1991, on the occasion of the Kalachakra initiation transmitted by His Holiness the Dalai Lama (teaching transcribed by Lotsawa Tenzin Dordjé), *Chö Yang,* no. 6 (journal). English text posted at: www.kalachakra.com/home/content/myth.html.

symbol of peace and great compassion. It is only with a certain peaceful awareness, steeped in love and compassion for all beings, that one can open to an understanding of what the kingdom of Shambhala really is. Essentially this means a state of pure consciousness.

If the art of Sengueï Ngaro is connected in this way to the kingdom of Shambhala—whether this connection is historical, artistic, philosophical, or spiritual—it is because Sengueï Ngaro can actually bring peace and well-being. It reconciles and harmonizes, and increases love, compassion, joy, and equanimity.

Just as in Shambhala, it is said that, through the benefits of the practice of Kalachakra, arguments can be transformed into agreements and conflicts into peaceful situations. So too, through the practice of Sengueï Ngaro, you can truly transform suffering into happiness, various disturbing emotions into wisdom, what is impure into what is pure, and even anger into compassion.

If you practice the art of Sengueï Ngaro with confidence and motivation, you will experience that on your own. Your understanding must be not only intellectual; you must come to understand Sengueï Ngaro through practicing it.

In fact there are very deep and secret links between the art of Sengueï Ngaro and the Shambhala kingdom, in particular with the Rigden kings; but this cannot be spoken of in a book. It is part of the oral transmission of Sengueï Ngaro, and its transmission depends very much on the capability of the practitioner to receive this kind of teaching. This is the difference between a warrior and a lama warrior, and between martial art and martial wisdom.

THE RIGDEN KINGS

It has been predicted that following the first king there will be a succession of seven kings and twenty-five holders of the caste title of *rigden*. At the present time we are at the twenty-first, named Chögyal Magakpa, or Aniruddha. It is said that he is seated on a throne of gold supported by lions, the same lions that are the emblem of Sengueï Ngaro.

According to predictions, at the time of the last king—Dragpo Chakkhorchen, "the powerful and ferocious king who brandishes a wheel of iron in his hand," also called Rudra Chakrin, "Rudra of the Wheel"—this king and his two sons, Tsangpa and Lhawang, will subjugate all the negative forces of the universe.

On Tibetan thangkas, Dragpo Khorlo is most often represented as riding a white horse and piercing his enemies with his lance. Sometimes he is accompanied by his general, Hanuman, who rides a dark blue horse.

He symbolizes the awakened activity of a bodhisattva who preserves and safeguards the teaching of the dharma. He is also considered to be a *dharmapala,* a protector struggling against negativity and piercing destructive forces with his lance. This is the manifestation of the adamantine wrath of the rulers of Shambhala.

This king is represented at the head of his armies, reestablishing order and harmony. These various armies represent the immeasurable forces of the great compassion, called "the four immeasurables." (See chapter 4.) This struggle is not a physical battle where there's an enemy to annihilate, but rather a spiritual transformation where ignorance is slain with the lance of the nondual wisdom of the Buddhas.

CHAPTER ELEVEN

LING
GESAR

THE LEGEND

King Ling Gesar is associated with the martial art of Sengueï Ngaro as a symbol of the warrior of Awakening, who slays negativity wherever it manifests. Even if this negativity takes the form of giants, monsters, or harmful genies, this kind of combat—both physical and spiritual—is actually only the mythic representation of martial activity of an awakened master for the welfare of beings. In reality, the legendary victories of King Ling Gesar simply emphasize the essential mission of all bodhisattvas: to quell injustice and violence and to have order reign on earth.

Throughout the long history of Ling Gesar, he has been considered to be a lama warrior or a kind of protector. The tradition of this king is found especially in Tibet, in the region of Kham, where the hero was born, but also in Mongolia among the Buriats. During the *losar* festivities that take place in Lhasa, you can observe the participants riding their magnificent horses. These riders, called *ndzong-ngyab zham-bo,* were considered to be the warriors of Gesar.

According to Tibetan tradition, Ling Gesar is considered to be a protector and conveys magic power to those who invoke him. This legendary king, sometimes called Ling Gyal (the King of Ling), is associated with a bodhisattva, sometimes even a mahasiddha.

The story of this warrior of Awakening was sung in Tibet by bards who told how the king descended from the sky to bring a reign of justice and peace to the earth. This descent to earth explains partially the name Emperor of Ling, or Emperor of Dzambuling.* Since Dzambuling designates the terrestrial world in Tibetan cosmology, Ling Gesar symbolizes sovereignty over the terrestrial kingdom. Some people think of Ling as the designation of a particular region in Kham.

Ling Gesar chose the way of the bodhisattvas. After having waged innumerable heroic struggles against negative forces, legend tells us that he returned to heaven having accomplished his enlightened activities, and having sealed his sword of wisdom in the heart of a sacred mountain.

Various versions of the story of Ling Gesar's coming to earth are sung in Tibet. In summary, the legend recounts that the god Qormusta received a prediction from the Shakyamuni Buddha concerning a period of confusion that was to come about in the future and, for that reason, he had to send one of his sons to the earth. When Qormusta spoke of this to his children, the youngest among them declared that he wanted to carry out this task. Following his request, he was born on earth as King Gesar.

The story recounts the extraordinary exploits of this king against the terrible giant of the north, who was inflicting horrible suffering on the inhabitants. He also enjoyed renowned victories over the sovereign of China, who had established a despotic regime in the region, and defeated the three khans of Siraigol.

The epic struggles of Ling Gesar are symbols. He fought giants, monsters, and ogres by using numerous magical powers of transformation.

THE WARRIOR OF AWAKENING

There is a connection between Ling Gesar and Roudra Chakrin, since both slay negativity and wage spiritual combat against evil.

---

*The continent Dzambu or Dzambuling, in Sanskrit, Dambud Vipa, designates the southern continent, one of the four principal continents of our world.

There are three essential points in this:

First, the Kalkin Kings of Shambhala, such as Roudra Chakrin, are considered to be emanations of King Ling Gesar. Their activities are identical because they are warriors of Awakening who struggle against adversity on earth, so that peace may reign. According to the legend, Ling Gesar is said to have set out toward the north, leaving behind his mate; this is the direction of the mythical city of Shambhala, also called Tchang Shambhala, the city of the north. According to the legend, Roudra Chakrin, the twenty-fifth sovereign in the Shambhala lineage, is also described as waging battles in the north. The cloud of the dharma that is represented on the emblem of Yoga Tchouzar is also moving toward the north (since the cascade is facing east).

Second, these two personages are both mythical kings. The first, Ling Gesar, belongs to the distant past of Tibetan tradition; and the second, Roudra Chakrin, must, in the not too distant future, come to this world to reestablish order in an apocalyptic era. Both come from a mythical kingdom unknown on earth, and both participate in humanity's unfolding by transforming a state of war into a situation of justice and peace.

These two points show how very often Roudra Chakrin is equated to an extension of Ling Gesar. Certain texts even designate Hanuman, the general of Roudra Chakrin, as the reincarnation of King Ling Gesar.

Third, this bodhisattva, deeply imbued with love and compassion like Roudra Chakrin, still embodies a form of royal and universal protection for the Tibetan people today. Like the Buddhist lions, these two mythical kings are the definitive peace-bringers. This peace is often symbolized on certain Tibetan thangkas by the unicorn pairs basking at the heart of its kingdom.

When describing the various aspects of Ling Gesar, Mipham Namgyal declared: "In the future you will be the Rigden Roudra Chakrin." But much more than the sovereign of the kingdom

Shambhala, Ling Gesar was also known as the king of the Dralas, those who, through the unyielding wrathful activity of submission (*dra* in Tibetan), truly implement the gift of protection in order to save others and protect them from danger.

In this sense King Ling is also associated with the symbol of the snow lion, and most particularly to the art of Sengueï Ngaro, the lion's roar. Legend holds that it was winning a horse race that made him eligible to become king of the country; that this glorious ruler, henceforth depicted as a knight on horseback equipped with helmet and armor and the wielder of divine weapons like the sword of wisdom, actually adopted the name Ling Gesar. He was then named Great Lion of the World (Sengtchen Ling), or Great Lion with the Black Mane. This is because his activity as the protector of beings and his symbolic battle against aggression, dedicated to subjugating various enemies and kings located at the four corners of the world, directly links him to the lion that is the protector of the land of snow.

This boundless gift of protection and love offered by King Gesar is especially distinguished by his desire that all beings know happiness and find protection from suffering, war, and danger. This is illustrated by the very fact that Ling Gesar bestowed upon himself the title Sengtchen Norbu Dradul, which means "the great lion, jewel who grants wishes, he who tramples his enemies."

In fact, these connections between King Ling Gesar and Roudra Chakrin have contributed to the popularity of the epic of Ling Gesar and of the myth of Shambhala among the people of central Asia, particularly in Tibet and in the region of Kham.

These mythical kings symbolize the irate warrior kings who set about to subjugate negative forces and bring peace to the earth.

Both are also represented in Tibetan iconography as riding white horses. These horses, the one of Ling Gesar* as well as the one of

---

*This horse is sometimes called in Tibetan Tra-rkyang-rgad.

Roudra Chakrin, represent a magic force. This energy, *lung ta,* is part of the practices of Sengueï Ngaro.

In this book, you will find only two images of King Ling Gesar, but you can also see rare depictions of this mythic figure in Tibet. Some are kept in the temples devoted to the legendary monarch, who is called Gesar Lhakhang in Tibetan.*

---

*There is a temple devoted to Ling Gesar in Lhasa, to the southwest of the Potala, called Rtse Pho Brang by the Tibetans, probably erected at the end of the eighteenth century.

CHAPTER TWELVE

THE ADAMANTINE SWORD

THE SWORD OF WISDOM

A flaming sword is represented on the emblem of Sengueï Ngaro. Like the sword of Ling Gesar, this type of sword is said to possess magical powers.

In Tibet there used to be a metal forging art that went hand in hand with consecrating this kind of sword through a precise ritual. This particular ritual, which is very close to that of the Japanese blacksmiths used in the fabrication of katanas and that of the Balinese in the fabrication of kriss, sometimes lasted for several months and required advanced knowledge of alchemy and astrology.

The deity Dordjé Lekpa,* protector of the teachings of Dzogchen as well as a deity of the forge, is associated with the development of this type of sword. The Thirteenth Dalai Lama assigned Dordjé Lekpa an important status: specifically, he had the function of a protector deity.†

Drepung monastery upheld the tradition of Sengueï Ngaro and shared it with Ganden and Sera, these three being famous monasteries

---

*One of three guardians protecting Dzogchen, "The Grand Perfection"; principally the guardian of *samayas*—oaths and commitments.
†In Tibetan: Srang-nia, from the monastery of Drepung (Bras-Spungs), near Lhasa.

near Lhasa. Sera monastery owned an entire collection of armor, shields, and weapons. These arms were offered by great warriors before death, as a gesture of renunciation of the warrior arts in favor of the spiritual path. We can see also in the GönKang of the Matho Monastery in Ladakh, 108 warrior swords, put in the wall as an offering by these warriors.

There are several types of magical swords in the world. Some are part of human history; others are the stuff of legend. In Tibet, there are several stories on this topic. For example, it is said that one of the Tibetan monasteries had a sword that was identical to that belonging to the deity Djampel Yang. Once a year this sword was used in a special ritual. As it was taken from its scabbard, only the great lamas were able to contemplate its brilliance and predict the future with precision by discerning certain signs, sacred letters, or various Buddhas who spontaneously appeared reflected in the immaculate blade of this saber.

Another legend from central Tibet mentions the protector Mgar Ba Nagpo, the black smithy who is also called *mgar bar 'i mtsham can,* "he who bears the marks of the black smithy," who is also an expression of Dordjé Lekpa in the lamaist pantheon. He is said to have created an invincible sword charged with magical forces. It had unlimited power and was preserved in a monastery in the south of Tibet.

In the art of Sengueï Ngaro, this sword has a particular meaning. The sword of eternal knowledge overcomes the enemy in the three spheres. The double-edged sword of eternal fire severs dualist illusions and subjugates the demons of emotion, and with its blazing fire delivers immediate comprehension and realization of transcendent wisdom. In brandishing this adamantine sword of immutability, the practitioner of Sengueï Ngaro enjoys the supreme knowledge of ultimate power.

The adamantine sword has several meanings and its symbolism is not revealed to the practitioner until he is capable of handling such a weapon, and of understanding the mysteries linked to various spiritual practices.

- It is called "the sword of eternal knowledge" because it has the power to set aside all that is of the domain of birth and death by extinguishing the fire of the passions and dissipating the darkness born of error.

- It is also called the sword that overcomes the enemy. It vanquishes the enemy of the three external spheres—form, formlessness, and desire; and the three internal spheres, the three poisons bound to the body, to words, and to the mind: desire or attachment, anger or aversion, and ignorance. These three spheres are reputed to be the enemy since they lead to death. The sword of eternal knowledge overcoming the enemy is identical to the sword of the unique hero Mahavajrabhairava (he who exterminates death).

- It is called a double-edged sword because this kind of sword is more like a broadsword than a saber. Its blade is straight and it cuts on both sides. It is said to be double-edged since it slices through subject–object duality that is linked to the three fundamental harmful tendencies, the three internal spheres. It allows one to go beyond illusion and negativity, removing obstacles from the path of the warrior of Awakening. Such a sword is identical to that of the protector of the lamaist pantheon Mahakala Chachikpa (the large black figure with four arms).

- It is also called the sword of eternal fire, since it has the power to drive out evil spirits and to remove obstacles that oppose the coming of Buddhas. It brings the adversaries of Buddhism into submission by frightening them with displays of martial dance. This kind of sword, said to be of eternal fire, is identical to that of Guru Rinpoche (the one who taught Pema Lingpa how to subdue demons with this sword).

- It is also called the sword that subdues the demons of the emotions, since even though it inspires a sacred terror, it represents the unruffled composure of the warrior of Awakening at the center of surrounding passions. It is a symbol of the naga king, who, in the form of an irritated dragon, immobilizes the point of his adversary's sword in his steely teeth and disarms him by seizing the blade in his claws. The sword that subdues the demons of the emotions is identical to the critical sword of the white naga king, Kulika, the king who has thirty squires and who resides in the northwest of the mandala of the naga kings.*

- This sword of wisdom is a flaming broadsword of immediate understanding that goes beyond concepts, since it is the fruit of penetrating direct vision, called *lhaktong* in Tibetan. This knowledge sees the ultimate nature of phenomena as emptiness. This is why it represents the dharma, not as a scriptural teaching (represented by a book in Tibetan iconography) but as the dharma of realization through inner and immediate experience.
- This sword is also compared to the unyielding sword of immutability. Being identical to the sword of the protector Miyowa, a specific guardian of Senguëi Ngaro, this sword is that of the king of the wrathful deities, Trogiel Miyo (he who is unshakable in his anger).
- This sacred sword also designates the sword of the supreme knowledge of ultimate power for the person who enjoys it, because, in slicing through the three spheres, the "sword of ordinary power" is sublimated into a "sword of ultimate power." Such a sword is identical to the sword of Mahasiddha Khadgapa (he who brandishes the sword).

All these various explanations of the symbolism concern the multitude of attributes and powers that this sword of wisdom has. In addition, there is an ultimate explanation about this sacred sword, but this teaching is mainly about how to handle it and the art of using it in a skillful way in the practices of Yoga Tchouzar.

THE SWORD OF THE BODHISATTVA

What differentiates the sword of wisdom from just any sword is the art of handling it. Obtaining such a sword is not ensured by merit, bravery,

---

*In Sanskrit: *nagaraja,* nine raga kings who are said to reside in the environs of eight provinces of the kingdom of Shambala, mainly in the rivers that separate the eight provinces of the country, as well as in its center.

virtues, noble blood, race, or origin. Only a bodhisattva initiated into ascetic practices and the perfection of transcendent wisdom can brandish such a weapon.

There are two kinds of sword: the ordinary warrior's sword and the sword of wisdom of the bodhisattva.*

The ordinary sword is the one the warrior uses in his search for power, victory, and absolute invincibility over his adversaries. This is the sword that the hero must steal or seize to use in battle and overcome his enemies. Or it may be inherited from his ancestors and from his master at arms. Such a sword, then, is a symbol of sovereignty over the material world, the indisputable sign of royalty, warrior-like heroism, and manly valor.

Most often dripping in blood, it remains, in spite of everything, the precious object of mystical cavaliers and of certain secret martial arts schools that think they can conquer purity, renunciation, and self-denial when fully armed.

The adamantine sword,† on the other hand, is under no circumstance a weapon intended to be used in war, to take life, or to conquer terrestrial kingdoms. The blade of such a sword is forged in an amalgam of eight to ten precious metals, often including metal from a meteorite. It has a unique sparkling blade, very heavy but at the same time light, and very strong but at the same time supple. Its manufacture follows an extremely precise ritual and takes place under distinct conditions. It is made for a particular person, traditionally for a master of Sengueï Ngaro.

The sacred sword of Sengueï Ngaro is similar to that of Djampel Yang, but its form is slightly different. In fact, there is a spiritual link connecting the sword of Djampel Yang, that of Roudra Chakrin, and the sword of Sengueï Ngaro. According to legend, the sacred sword was kept at the monastery of Utse, and was venerated as if it were the very

---

Bodhisattva means literally "the one who struggles with courage for the good of beings."

†In Sanskrit: *khadga vajra.*

sword of Djampel Yang. In this monastery, which also houses a precious statue of Djampel Yang and his holy books, the sword is carefully preserved.

Such a sword is represented also in the possession of the future king of Shambhala, Roudra Chakrin. The twenty-fifth of the royal lineage, this king represents a reincarnation of the bodhisattva Djampel Yang, riding a white horse and armed with the sword of a bodhisattva.

According to the teachings of my master, such swords have been forged on several occasions in Tibet. They have been considered to be just as precious as the swords of Ling Gesar or of the bodhisattva Djampel Yang. Their power is greater than that of an ordinary sword. A lama described the magical power of the sword of Ling Gesar to Alexandra David-Néel as follows: "The sword can be symbolic. Its blade can emit invisible sparks that will penetrate people's minds and transform them."[1]

Conclusion

I have set forth these few teachings for all those who wish one day to receive the transmission of Sengueï Ngaro in order to be able to practice it, or for those who simply want to study the history and specific philosophy of this cultural tradition of Tibet in order to understand it better.

This book is a modest account of the struggle undertaken to safeguard this tradition as homage to my teacher, Lama Tra, who devoted almost his entire life to preserving this heritage, respecting *The Eleven Vessels of Nectar,* the code of ethics of Sengueï Ngaro.

From the bottom of my heart, I wish that this record will pass on to future generations a trace of the living wisdom of the lama warriors of the past, and encourage them to transmit this flame so that it is not extinguished.

Following the example of the lama warriors, the martial art of Sengueï Ngaro teaches us a veritable art of living so that peace and love can take root in all hearts. Uniting right and spontaneous action with the compassion and wisdom of the Buddhas is the only path to follow in mastering this art of the "warrior of Awakening," or bodhisattva. The practitioner of Sengueï Ngaro, then, must work for a springing forth in his heart of the great cascade of bodhicitta, "so that the flames of anger might be extinguished," because perfecting the absolute mastery of the martial arts forms cannot be accomplished without engendering bodhicitta.

However, much more than a martial art, the "roaring of the lion" supports the liberation of beings from ignorance, lethargy, and hatred. For this, the true lama warrior must first confront himself. If he manages to gain mastery over his own mind, he will become the conqueror of duality and illusion. As a messenger of peace, he will be able to enter into the great work of the legendary king Ling Gesar, who sunders negativity wherever it appears.

> *May the roaring of the lion resonate throughout the*
>   *entire universe!*
> *May the hearts of beings open to love and compassion.*
> *May each of us live in inner peace!*

The Eleven Vessels of Nectar

By tuning in, contemplation, and practicing Sengueï Ngaro cultivating the spirit of Awakening: in striving to protect individuals without harming others, practicing without respite to strengthen one's patience and, while maintaining mental calm, spread the Transcendent Wisdom for the good of all beings.

Through the protection of others, one's own training, and the teaching of Sengueï Ngaro implementing the spirit of Awakening: by skillfully using its various profound, secret, ultimate, and excellent techniques for the good of all beings.

By becoming a student, instructor, then master of Sengueï Ngaro never departing from the spirit of Awakening: by learning, by accomplishing and then by transmitting Sengueï Ngaro both partially and in its entirety, based on the abilities and skills of each individual for the good of all beings.

Never practice Sengueï Ngaro to challenge others, to take the measure of others against your own, to use any kind of weapon, to fight with the intention of hurting another or waging war, but solely for the good of all beings.

Never practice Sengueï Ngaro for your own personal profit, for glory or renown, or in a spirit of competition, but solely for the good of all beings.

Never practice Sengueï Ngaro to enrich yourself, to increase your power or to obtain power over others, but principally for the good of all beings.

Never distort Sengueï Ngaro, alter it, or blend it with other arts, blend it with another discipline or omit any of its teachings, but only enrich this cultural tradition of Tibet for the good of all beings.

Never reveal Sengueï Ngaro to those who are not engaged in its practice, or to individuals foreign to the instruction and ethical code of the Lama warriors, or greedy to possess certain teachings without wishing to put them in practice solely for the good of all beings.

Never knowingly use or transmit Sengueï Ngaro for evil purpose, by seeking to go beyond ones abilities and skills, by transgressing the various levels of apprenticeship and teaching, or by violating the rules, or by concealing the code of ethics, or by profaning the art of Sengueï Ngaro, but solely for the good of all beings.

Never teach Sengueï Ngaro to those displaying bad conduct, who belong to sects, or who act outside the law, but solely for the good of all beings.

Never teach Sengueï Ngaro without conforming fully with the rules of this art, the teachings of the lineage, and to the pedagogy, discipline, and ethical code specific to Sengueï Ngaro in order the transmission retains its purity, force, and benediction for the good of all beings.

WRITTEN BY YOGI TCHOUZAR PA,
the fifteenth day of the eleventh month
of the year of the Water Horse in order for
the teachings of the Lion's Roar to be
for the good of all others

ACKNOWLEDGMENTS

I am grateful to all those who contributed to the preparation and production of this book.

In particular to the teachers of Tibetan Buddhism, those from Tibet's glorious past as well as today's guardians of the flame of wisdom: some encouraged me; others inspired me or transmitted teachings of great value.

I want to especially thank my friends and members of the Sengueï Ngaro Association who have contributed directly or indirectly to these teachings: for the drawing of animals and for rereading the manuscript and the two lions Kouthoumi and Jérémie.

Anyone wishing to study and practice Sengueï Ngaro can contact
The Association Sengueï Ngaro
c/o ABC DOM
16, rue Foncet
06000 Nice, France
Telephone +33620429358
Website: www.sengueingaro.fr

GLOSSARY

bodhisattva: Literally, "he who struggles with courage for the welfare of beings." A bodhisattva accomplishes the six Buddhist "perfections" and develops the four "immeasurables" in order to acquire the Buddha state. There are two kinds of bodhisattva: terrestrial and transcendent. A terrestrial bodhisattva has not accomplished the perfection of wisdom, but his capacity for taking on the suffering of others allows him to develop an immutable compassion through his thoughts, words, and actions. A transcendent bodhisattva has already come to the perfection of wisdom and has attained the Buddha state: his infinite love extends to all beings and his compassion is of limitless intensity.

bodhicitta: The spirit of Awakening. On the relative level, this corresponds to the desire to obtain perfect Awakening for the welfare of all beings. Since it is relative, it comes into being supported by thought. On an absolute level, it refers to wisdom in which the movement of thought is consolidated.

dharma: This word has several meanings. There are three principal ones:

- The body of teachings of the Buddha and of enlightened beings that shows the path toward Awakening.
- Any phenomenon or thing that occupies a moment of existence. *Dharma* means "grasp, hold, support, protect." Because they have their own identity, all things are dharma.
- Truth, ultimate reality, the real mode of being of things as the Buddha taught.

There are two aspects: the dharma of the texts, which refers to the support of these teachings; and the dharma of enlightenment, which is the result of spiritual practice.

dharmadhatu: The emptiness inherent in awakened consciousness.

disturbing emotions: Those that cloud the true nature of the mind. Traditionally five principal emotions are identified: desire, anger, ignorance, jealousy, and pride.

the four elements: Earth, water, fire, and air.

geshe: An abbreviation of Gewe Shenyen, meaning "friend in virtue." In the *Sutrayana,* this term designates the spiritual master. This title "doctor of divinity" requires about twenty years of practice in meditation, study, and retreat.

kalpa: A cosmic era. A *great kalpa* designates the duration of a universe, from the moment it begins to form until the moment it returns to nothingness. A kalpa is divided into twenty-four "small kalpas." An "intermediate kalpa" corresponds to a small kalpa during which the duration of a life increases and another during which it decreases.

karma: Literally "action," the act and the mental energy that it engenders; the physical, verbal, or mental act and its effect. Karma obeys two basic laws:

- You never undergo the consequences of an act that you have not completed.
- The force of an act is never exhausted until it has produced its effect, unless it is neutralized by an appropriate remedy.

klesha: One of the veils that hide the real and prevent total Awakening from being achieved. There are two main kinds: the veil of emotions—designating the five poisons: ignorance, desire, anger, jealousy, and pride—which is an obstacle to liberation from *samsara;* and the veil of cognition—belief in the reality of oneself and in phenomena—masking the ultimate knowledge of all things and being an obstacle to omniscience.

lama: Honorific title given to scholarly and practiced spiritual masters. The term is often used for religious figures in general. This word comes from the Tibetan *la na me pa,* which means "unsurpassable," and *ma,* which means "mother." The word *lama* alludes to the qualities and compassion that a mother has for her unique child.

Mara: Personification of all the obstacles that the practitioner will encounter on the path of Awakening.

nirvana: Literally, "beyond suffering." This term has different meanings in the different vehicles of the teaching, and designates several levels of Awakening.

Oddiyana: The land of *dakinis* where Guru Rinpoche was born. It is located between present-day Afghanistan and Kashmir.

penetrating vision: Perception of the ultimate nature of phenomena.

Rigden: Title of the kings of Shambhala.

samsara: Cycle of successive existences in which living beings experience various forms of suffering engendered by ignorance and the emotions. This involves the circle of death and rebirth in which beings pass without interruption from one life to another, impelled by the force of their own acts (karma). It is characterized mainly by impermanence and suffering.

terma: System of transmission of esoteric teachings revealed by the discoverers of treasures, called *tertons,* in the form of treasures of the dharma (profound teachings, statues, ritual objects, remedies, and so on). These treasures were hidden in sacred places by enlightened beings, then rediscovered in the appropriate era.

thangka: Traditional Tibetan painting most often representing a specific iconography. Thangkas are produced following precise instructions preserved in manuscripts of the Buddhist tradition. Tibetan scholars believe that the word *thangka* comes from *than-yig,* a Tibetan expression meaning "remembrance of facts or events." Thangkas are painted on silk, or occasionally on cotton.

Vajrayana: The adamantine vehicle, also called Tantrayana or Mantrayana, one of the names of the tantric teachings and practices of Buddhism. *Vajra* means diamond, that which is indestructible. *Yana* means "vehicle" or "means": the direct and very skillful means in order to attain the supreme goal of Awakening. Because these teachings are practiced secretly and are not intended for those not suited to receive them, this vehicle is also called the "secret mantras."

wisdom: The awakened consciousness that has always been present naturally in the mental current of all beings.

ABOUT THE COLOR
ILLUSTRATIONS

The Sengueï Ngaro Buddha (plate 4)

Above this rare painting depicting the "Roar of the Lion" Buddha resting upon a lotus is the high-realized lama Djé Tsongkhapa, in order to provide a reminder that he would reappear in the form of this eleventh Buddha. This thangka was consecrated by several Geshes including the most senior Gueshe, Lobsang Gyeltsen (ninety-one years old), Geshe Tséwang Dordjé, and the Venerable Jetsun Rigdzin Tcheuzang of Shugseb Gompa. His Holiness Gyalwang Karmapa personally put his signature on it, thereby giving his blessing to the activity of the martial art Sengueï Ngaro in order to forge its sacred bond with this very distinctive Buddha who bears the same name. So that great benefits would not be long in coming, a Tibetan inscription was written in calligraphy on the back by the Venerable Ngawang Tséring of Sabo Gompa.

Séngtchèn Norbu Dradul (plate 5)

Thangka, Tibet, seventeenth century, 28 × 36 cm

A rare depiction of King Gesar Ling surrounded by wrathful manifestations intended to vanquish his enemies: a fire-spitting scorpion equipped with multiples eyes of wisdom intended to defeat the "Gyalpos," a white yak devouring its enemies . . . The upper part of the painting reminds us that in ancient times, Gesar was the Omniscient Guru Rinpoche, here seated on a lotus throne surrounded by rainbows. The lower portion of the painting retraces the extraordinary origins of this hero: his father, a native of the divine land of the Lha, was named Singlen and his mother Gogmo, a native of the underground kingdom of the Nagas, was half woman and half serpent. A number of Jewels That Grant Wishes are emerging from the water and peacefully resting unicorn couples recall the overflowing state of nonviolence and compassion that rules in Ling's country. This is a peace maintained by the activity of King Gesar, here magnificently represented on his horse in royal harness, galloping through space.

Djampel Yang (plate 6)

Thangka, Tibet, eighteenth century, 15 × 20 cm

This representation of Djampel Yang personifies the wisdom of the Buddhas. Somewhat orange in color, he is seated in the diamond posture, holding in one hand the sword of wisdom and the book of transcendent knowledge and in the other the bow and arrow.

This bodhisattva, who confers the intelligence of all-penetrating knowledge of the teachings of the Buddha and his commentators, induces excellent qualities and erudition.

Guru Rinpoche (plate 7)

Gilded bronze, Tibet, sixteenth century, 14 cm

Considered equal to a Buddha, he was revered by the order of ancient ones, the Nyingmapa, as The Second Buddha. He is also called Padmasambhava, "he who is born from the lake, who has sprung forth from the lotus." Having arisen in a mythical land, this lord of Oddiyana was a great ascetic and a magician. He built the first Tibetan monastery of Samye in the eighth century, and ordained the first monks there. This statue represents him in an unusual way, with a headdress very similar to that of warrior-kings such as Ling Gesar, wearing boots and a cape with broad sleeves and holding a *khatavanga*-mother and a dordjé in front of the heart.

Ling Gesar Herouka (plate 8)

Thangka, Tibet, seventeenth century, 35 × 53 cm

Rare representation of King Ling Gesar in a wrathful aspect. He brandishes a bow and arrow, and also holds a scepter (*dordjé*) and a bell (*drilbu*). Above him are representations of Guru Rinpoche, the protector Tamdrin, and Chenrezi. Below him are two armed horsemen.

Notice the four mythological animals—the tiger, the snow lioness, the garuda, and the dragon. The dragon is relegated to the thangka border, accompanied by rainbows.

Dordjé Drolo (plate 9)

Tsakli, miniature painting on cotton, Tibet, eighteenth century, 8 × 11 cm

Wrathful form of Guru Rinpoche. Dancing on a tigress, he brandishes the dordjé in his right hand and the *phurba* in his left. He is accompanied by a garuda soaring above him. In this aspect, named "ferocious and adamantine," Guru Rinpoche hid numerous treasures (*terma*), while providing lists of them and predicting their discovery. Dordjé Drolo allows all impediments to be resolved and wards off external, internal, and secret obstacles. Through his veneration, illness, famine, and war are made to disappear.

Vajra Dakkini Herouka (plate 10)

Thangka, Tibet, seventeenth century, 58 × 40 cm

Rare representation of the Adamantine Yogini as she is described by Patrul Rinpoche in *The Way of the Great Perfection*: ". . . red in color, her face, arms, and legs are in a walking stance. Her three eyes look heavenward . . . and she wears a long necklace of flowers . . ." The Tibetan letter *A*, used in the practice called *powa*, is drawn discretely in the upper left part of the painting. An inscription by the painter, who must have been a practitioner of this type of "transfer of consciousness" practice, is to be found on the back of the thangka. It states, "How marvelous! Moving from the web of originless appearances, the divinity of the ultimate meaning and direction beneath the forms springs up freely and spontaneously—beneath these forms that are similar to those of the conquerors, extensions of their bodies, their words, and their awakened minds, which are respectively Vajrapani, Hayagriva, and Garuda; and through forms that are similar to the Vajra Dakini Heruka, mother of all the conquerors. When I drew them, the strength of my motivation and of my virtuous practice increased. In my next existence, may there be auspicious signs for being reborn in the paradise of the conquerors. May happy omens shine brightly!"

Nechung Dordjé Drakden (plate 11)

Tibetan painting, seventeenth century, 21 × 17 cm

Guardian spirit of the earth who opposed the construction of the Samye monastery in the eighth century, and who was conquered by Guru Rinpoche. This form, which represents the leader of the earth genies or kings (*gyalpo* in Tibetan), is also identified with the red protector Pehar Gyalpo. The Gelug lineage assigns Pehar Gyalpo to the highest level of protector deities. Since the time of the great fifth Dalai Lama, he has been declared the official protector of the Tibetan government. He was especially venerated by the lineage of Panchen Lamas and Dalai Lamas.

His principal function is to subdue hostile forces. He is seated on a white snow lioness, has six arms and three heads, and is bedecked with a headdress called *theh-shu*.

Deouatchen (plate 12)

Thangka, Tibet, eighteenth century, 43 × 48 cm

This painting represents the Buddha Opame, called in Sanskrit Amithaba, or infinite light. At its center, in a magnificent palace surrounded by fabled trees and beneficent springs, beams the lord of the pure field of felicity, which is the color of rubies. On his right is the bodhisattva of great compassion (Chenrezi) and on his left, the bodhisattva of great power (Tchana Dordjé) surrounded by innumerable bodhisattvas.

Represented in several places in the painting, the Opame Buddha intervenes to help those who have invoked him; he protects beings from the threats of fire and water.

This paradise, called Dewatchen in Tibetan, shines with a rainbow light. We can see a little person being born, through the force of his devotion and his prayers, from the opening bud of a lotus. With his two hands brought together and his head turned toward the Opame Buddha, he represents the reality of awakening to the Buddha state as soon as the lotus opens.

Dukkhar Tchenma (plate 13)

Thangka, Tibet, seventeenth century, 54 × 74 cm

Representation of the Protectress with the White Parasol. Holding the parasol that flutters in the wind and is the symbol of increasing good fortune, she is the sign of supreme protection. With her help one can travel any road, free from danger. The ultimate protection is the attainment of emptiness. She crushes below her feet all obstacles—external, internal, and secret—represented in the form of weapons, evil genies, venomous and dangerous animals, supernatural monsters, and so on. She has a thousand faces and a thousand arms, while numerous eyes of wisdom cover her body.

Tchana Dordjé (plate 14)
Thangka, Tibet, seventeenth century, 76 × 58 cm

Representation of the Maha-Bodhisattva of the tenth land named Tchana Dordjé, one of the three great bodhisattvas of the Sambhogakaya, along with Tchenrezi and Djampel Yang. In his right hand he brandishes a dordjé, the diamond scepter, showing that he possesses the power and mind of all Buddhas. The Buddha Shakyamuni is represented above, among the flames of wisdom that emanate from the body of the protector. This spiritual power allows him to conquer negativity, a sign that the subtlest traces of ignorance of the ultimate nature of reality have been severed through the action of *samadhi* meditation, a meditation that is similar to Vajra meditation.

NOTES

CHAPTER 1

1. Dhagpo Kagyu Ling, *A Source of Benefit and Happiness* (Saint-Léon-sur-Vézère, France: The Library of Dhagpo Kagyu Ling, 2007).

CHAPTER 4

1. Teachings of Yogi Tchouzar Pa, extract from the collection *La Cascade des Chants Vajra* (The Cascade of Vajra Songs).
2. Dhagpo Kagyu Ling, *A Source of Benefit and Happiness.*
3. Translated from the French as cited in *Sur l'Océan du Mahayana,* by Lobsang Tengye Gueshé (Marzens, France: Éditions Vajra Yogini, 1993), 120.
4. Prophecy about the decadent age excerpted from a terma discovered by the great Terton Rigzin Jatson Nyingpo, entitled *Les Réponses de Gourou Rinpotché aux Questions de Nyang Wen* (Guru Rinpoche Answers the Questions of Nyang Wen). (Saint-Léon-sur-Vézère, France: Éditions Dhagpo Kagyu).

CHAPTER 9

1. Extract from the teaching collection *La Cascade des Chants Vajra.*
2. Chogyam Trungpa, *Shambhala: The Sacred Path of the Warrior* (Boston: Shambhala Publications, 1988).

CHAPTER 12

1. Alexandra David-Néel, *The Superhuman Life of Gesar of Ling* (Whitefish, Mont.: Kessinger Publishing, 2004), 270. David-Néel was a European student of theosophy and Buddhism who first visited Tibet in the early 1900s and subsequently authored or translated more than thirty books, primarily on Eastern religion and philosophy.

ABOUT THE AUTHOR

Yogi Tchouzar Pa is the last holder of the Lineage of the Dragpo Lamas of Tibet. Heir of Sengueï Ngaro, he received the ensemble of the profound, secret, ultimate, and excellent techniques from the last surviving master, Lama Tra. These techniques had been transmitted without interruption for nine generations.

In 1991, Yogi Pa earned a master of philosophy for his essay "The Budo and the Wisdom Paths of Japan." Since 1996, he has also instructed the law enforcement personnel in France. Founder of the Association of Sengueï Ngaro, he has participated since 1997 in the safeguarding of the traditional arts connected to Tibetan Buddhism. He also contributes to construction projects for the Shugseb monastery retreat center of the Venerable Jétsun Rigdzin Tcheuzang and to renovation work for the Venerable Lama Ngawang Tsering at Sabo in Ladakh.

Yogi Tchouzar Pa is the initiator of several programs and articles that have revealed all the richness concerning the martial, philosophical, artistic, and spiritual planes of Sengueï Ngaro. He has been invited all over the world to reveal and teach this misunderstood art, and he has founded numerous centers of Sengueï Ngaro in Europe and elsewhere.

Yogi Tchouzar Pa is the author of a complete work of Sengueï Ngaro and the seven booklets of techniques published by the Sengueï Ngaro Association. Yogi Pa has presented the techniques of Sengueï Ngaro at conferences, demonstrations, and on television.

He lives in France.

INDEX

accumulation, 82–83

adamantine sword, 181–86

adamantine wrath, 10

adversity, 68–70

aggression, 24, 46–47, 87–89, 92

agility, 21

agitation, 79, 145–46

air, 157–62

amchis, 16

anger, 38, 43, 54, 62–63, 67, 73, 86–89, 89–90, 132, 144–45

anointing of the bodhisattvas, 161–62

armor-clad effort, 75

Ashita, 8

attachment, 38, 87

attention, 76–78

attire, 141–42

Awakening, 15, 32, 62–63, 177–80

bear, 121–23

being, 92

bodhicitta, 25, 52

bodhisattva, 184–86

Bokar Rinpoche, Venerable, 103–4

branch falling to the ground, 112–13

breathing, 99–100, 106–7, 136–37

Buddha, pl.4, 8, 57, 72–73, 169–70, 195

Bui, Lama, 19–28, 66, 113

butterfly, 119, 127–28

cauldrons, 22–26

center, 93

Chögyal Magakpa, 174–75

Chogyam Trungpa, 157

chorten, 130–31

Chuan Pai, Lama, 18

cloud of impermanence, 158–59

cloud of the law, 159–61

cold anger, 88

compassion, 14–15, 43, 45, 48–51, 70, 86–89, 144–45

compound existences, 91–92

concentration, 76–79, 100

confrontation, 87

courage, 55, 69–70, 75

crab, 125

crane, pl.22–23, 124–25

cruelty, 25–26

Daidot, Lama, 6, 12, 16–17

Dalai Lama, 66, 70

David-Néel, Alexandra, 31, 188

death, 158

Deouatchen, pl.12

development, 13

Dhamchen Dordjé Lekpa, 11

dharma, 8

dharmachakra, 73–74

dharmapalas, 11, 142

dharma vinaya, 141–42

discipline, 59–66

discouragement, 43

distraction, 41–43

Djampel Yang, pl.6, 11, 182, 185–86, 196

Djé Tsongkhapa, 9

dohas, 152

Dordjé Drolo Tsakli, pl.9

Dordjé Lekpa, 181

doubt, 73, 146–47

dragon, 6, 98, 128, 129

Dragpo Chakkhorchen, 175

Dragpo Khorlo, 13, 175

Drukpa Kunley, 166

Dukhar Tchenma, pl.13, 56, 198–99

dullness, 79

Dun Dro Tchou, 81, 118–28

earth, 154–57

effort, 40–41, 70–76

ego, 70

eightfold path, 74

eight long movements, pl.20, 100–102

eight provinces, 168–69

eight short movements, pl.20, 100–102

Eight Verses on Training the Mind, 67

eighty-six movements, pl.15–17, 102–5

eleven vessels of nectar, 189–90

emotional instability, 87–88

emptiness, 81–82, 93–96

enemies, 69–70

energy, 41, 134–35

enthusiasm, 74–75

ethical discipline, 59–66

evil, 24, 60–61, 63–64

exchange, 45–48

Expansion of the Great Realization, 85

fame, 73

familiarization, 86

fear, 25, 53, 73

fearlessness, 55, 78

fire, 162–66

fisherman lama, 109–16

five animals, form of, 129–35

five elements, 135, 169. *See also* four
    elements

five obstacles, 78–79

flag, 130

Flame of Wisdom, 26–27

flexibility, 116

forgetting instructions, 79

form of eight movements that empty and
    the eight movements that fill, 117

form of eighty-six movements, pl.15–17,
    102–5

form of the fisherman lama, 109–16

form of the five animals, 129–35

form of the forty-two palms of the
    Buddha, pl.18–19, 105–7

form of the ten animals, pl.20–25,
    121–28

form of the ten circles, pl.26, 135–38
forty-two palms of the Buddha,
    pl.18–19, 105–7
four elements
    air, 157–62
    earth, 154–57
    fire, 162–66
    water, 150–54
Four Immeasurables, 48, 51, 175
friends, 78

Gampopa, 83–85
Gangten Tulku Rinpoche, His
    Eminence, 90
garuda, 6, 129
generosity, 53–59
gentleness, 132, 135
Gesar, Ling, 6
Geshe Langri Thangpa, 67
Geshe Ngawang Tashi, 170, 173
giving, 47–48, 53–59
glass of water exercise, 147–49
Golden Chopsticks, 20–22
great waterfall of bodhicitta, 150
Guendune Rinpoche, Very Venerable
    Lama, 15
Guendun Rinpoche, Venerable Lama, 62
guru drap kilaya, 14
gyalpos, 14–15
Gyalwang Drukpa, His Holiness the
    Twelfth, 89
Gyalwang Karmapa, 8–9
Gyalwang Namkhai Norbu, 14–15

happiness, 71
His Master's Only Praise, 27–28

honor, 73
horseback posture, 98
hot anger, 88
Hsing Lung, 18
humility, 75–76
hunger, 73
hypocrisy, 73

ignorance, 38, 94
impermanence, 43, 77, 90–91, 158–59
imperturbability, 75
indolence, 73, 145
insatiable effort, 76
inseminating island, 156–57
intelligence, 81
intervention, 79
Iron Ball Wrapped in Silk, 22
irrevocable determination, 75

jalu, 32
jealousy, 38, 87
Jetsun Taranatha, 173
Jewel Ornament of Liberation, The, 55,
    83–84
joyous effort, 75–76

Kalachakra texts, 169–72
Kalu Rinpoche, His Holiness, pl.7, pl.9,
    44, 53, 54, 87, 172, 196, 197
karma, 22–26
khampa warriors, 6, 16–17, 141–42
Khamtrul Rinpoche, Venerable, 173
khandro, 11
Khatok Rigdzin Tchenpo, Venerable,
    165–66
killing, 24, 65–66

kindness, 25–26

kleshas, 159

Korde rushen, 119–20

ksar, 140

Kyabje Yongdzin Trijang Rinpoche, His
    Holiness, 170

Labdrön, Machik, 30

lack of effort, 40–41

lama warriors, 13–15, 141–42

Lao Tzu, 68

laughter, 28

laziness, 72, 73, 79, 145

leaky container, 38

lechery, 73

lethargy, 145

Ling Gesar, King, pl.5, pl.8, 176–80,
    186, 195–97

Lingpa, Jigme, 12

lions, 12, 78

lion throne, 6–7

loathing, 73

love, 43, 70

lung ta, 129

Mahakala Chachikpa, 183

Mahasiddha Khadgapa, 184

malevolence, 24–25

mamos, 14

mandalas, 18, 168

Mara, 72–73

marigpa, 94

mastery, 13

meditation, 25, 83–84, 143–47

mental dispersion, 76–77

meridians, 136

merit, 85

Meru, Mount, 155–56

Mgar Ba Nagpo, 182

Milarepa, 69

Mipham Namgyal, 178–79

miyowa, 68

mongoose, pl.21, 119, 124

monkey, 126

motivation, 59, 104

nag thank, 142

nature, 151

Nechung Dordjé Drakden, 11, pl.11

negativity, 68

ngaro, 9

noncompound, 91–92

nonintervention, 79

nonviolence, 66

nonvirtuous actions, 24–26

nothingness, 136

obstacle mountain, 156

Opame Buddha, pl.12, 198

opening, 78

Orgyenpa, 173

overturned container, 38

pacification, 13

Padmasambhava, 11

patience, 66–70

pawo, 11

Pelden Yeshe, 171

perfect action, 78

periphery, 93

perseverance, 74–75

poison-filled container, 38

praise, 27–28, 73

Prajnaparamita, 82–83

praying mantis, 119, 125–26

*Precious Rosary of the Warrior of
     Awakening,* 40–41

pride, 27–28, 38, 39, 87

protection, 53–59, 72

punishment, 22–26

Punishment with Two Cauldrons,
     22–26

rainbow body, 32

refuge island, 154–55

restraint, 60–61

rgyas pa. *See* development

Rigden kings, 174–75

Rigdzin Tcheuzang, Venerable, 28–33

right action, 74

right concentration, 74

right effort, 73–74, 74

right intention, 74

right livelihood, 74

right mindfulness, 74

right view, 74

rigorous effort, 75

rigpa, 94

rinpoches, 11, 16

roaring, 78

Roaring Lion, 8–9

rolling up of the serpent, 112

Roudra Chakrin, 177–80, 185

samara, 21, 41

Sangye thelmo cheunyi, 105–7

scorn, 73

self-absorption, 43

self-mastery, 145

Séngtchèn Norbu Dradul, pl.5

Sengué Dradrok, 11

senguei, 6–7

Sengueï Ngaro, 6–7
     adamantine wrath and, 10
     flag of, 130
     founder of, 16–17
     lineage of, 17–18
     roar of truth and, 7–9

serenity, 95

seven flames, 164–65

Shambhala, 13, 103–4, 168–75

shinay, 77

shunyata, 91

six stains, 39–44

six transcendent perfections, 52, 84–85
     concentration, 76–79
     effort, 70–76
     ethical discipline, 59–66
     gift of protection, 53–59
     patience, 66–70
     transcendent wisdom, 80–86

snake, 127

snow lioness, pl.3, 6, pl.24, 129, 132

Sönam, 31

Song of the Great Adamantine Cascade,
     153–54

Song of the Lotus Rosary, 107–9

Sound of the Bell, 27

spirals, 105

spirits, 14–15

spiritual poisons, 38

staff, 48–51, 109–16

standing meditation, 98–100

steadfastness, 75

steady effort, 75

strength, 21, 130–34

Suddhodana, 8

suffering, 61, 68, 77

swords, 181–86

Tashi Tseringma, 11

Tchana Dordjé, 10, 11, pl.12, pl.14, 199

tchou, 140

Tchouzar yoga, 74, 80, 81, 94, 140–41, 168

teachings of Lama Bui, 20–28

techniques

    eight long movements, pl.20, 100–102

    eight short movements, pl.20, 100–102

    form of eighty-six movements, pl.15–17, 102–5

    form of the fisherman lama, 109–16

    form of the five animals, 129–35

    form of the forty-two palms of the Buddha, pl.18–19, 105–7

    form of the ten animals, pl.20–25, 121–28

    form of the ten circles, pl.26, 135–38

    glass of water exercise, 147–49

    meditation, 143–47

    standing meditations, 98–100

Tempa Gyamtso, 28–30

ten animals, pl.20–25, 121–28

ten circles, form of, pl.26, 135–38

tenth land, 161–62

thangkas, 7

thirst, 73

Thirty-Seven Bodhisattva Practices, 43, 46

thögyal, 32

three circles, 58

three defaults of the container, 37–39

Tibet, 19–20

tiger, 6, pl.25, 118, 119, 123, 129

Tilopa, 67

tonglen, 45–48

Tra, Lama, 10, 18, 58, 61, 94, 106, 109–10, 131, 146

transcendent wisdom, 80–86

Trogiel Miyo, 184

truth, 7–9

tshad med bzhi, 51

Tsong Khapa, Venerable Lama, 63

tummo, 165–66

vajra anger, 10

Vajra Dakkini Herouka, pl.10, 197

vigorous effort, 75

violent subjugation, 13–15

virtue, 72

vital energy, 134–35

vital points, 64–65

water, 150–54

wealth, 56–57

wind horse, 129

Window of the Sun, 98

wisdom, 80–86, 130–34, 163–64, 181–84

wooden posts, 131

zhiba. *See* pacification

BOOKS OF RELATED INTEREST

The Spiritual Practices of the Ninja
Mastering the Four Gates to Freedom
by Ross Heaven

Martial Arts Teaching Tales of Power and Paradox
Freeing the Mind, Focusing Chi, and Mastering the Self
by Pascal Fauliot

Nei Kung
The Secret Teachings of the Warrior Sages
by Kosta Danaos

The Martial Arts of Ancient Greece
Modern Fighting Techniques from the Age of Alexander
by Kostas Dervenis and Nektarios Lykiardopoulos

Aikido and Words of Power
The Sacred Sounds of Kototama
by William Gleason

The Spiritual Foundations of Aikido
by William Gleason

Shaolin Qi Gong
Energy in Motion
by Shi Xinggui

The Warrior Is Silent
Martial Arts and the Spiritual Path
by Scott Shaw, Ph.D.

Inner Traditions • Bear & Company
P.O. Box 388
Rochester, VT 05767
1-800-246-8648
www.InnerTraditions.com

Or contact your local bookseller